SATTIC LIFESTYLE OF THE TAMILS

SAMAYAL in Tamil just means to cook a meal.

ANNAM, food, is a type of the Almighty (annam parabrahma swaroopam) as per the Hindu sacred texts. All creatures conceived are supported on food and eventually return to the earth and converge with it to become food. Food is the preeminent medication of all (aushadham ucchyate sarvam).

Food possesses a significant part in the existences of Hindus. Food is proposed to progenitors during customs, to Gods during strict functions and to gods in the sanctuaries. Food is served to poor people and the destitute as seva or beneficent help; to creatures and birds as strict obligation; to one's very own god prior to eating to kill destructive energies contained in the food. Youngsters are instructed not to disregard or reject food; householders are informed to store bounty regarding food and to engage their atithis or visitors with anything food has been cooked that very day.

The Hindu lifestyle likewise lays accentuation on eating the right sort of food - the principle wellspring of energy for the actual body. The food that we eat directly affects the three characteristics of sathva, *rajas and tamas in our bodies*. This thus, impacts the surplus of our psyches and bodies.

The player for tiffin was ground in an aatukal or a mortar and pestle. Kindling was the essential fuel in dim kitchens. The vessels utilized for cooking required steady consideration, and were scoured and cleaned utilizing tamarind skin and debris. Also the scouring brush was the fiber of the coconut. It was eco-accommodating and far superior than the present scotch-brite. Also not at all like as in a scotch-brite this coconut fiber didn't hurt the nails or the fingers. Those were the days indeed.

Most fixings were new, obtained from rural grounds and gardens at the backs of homes. Tamarind, banana, mango, lime, drumsticks and coconut trees filled nearby. Produce from these trees tracked down its direction into the food. Vegetables were likewise planted in the terrace; with some, the yield was seasonal.

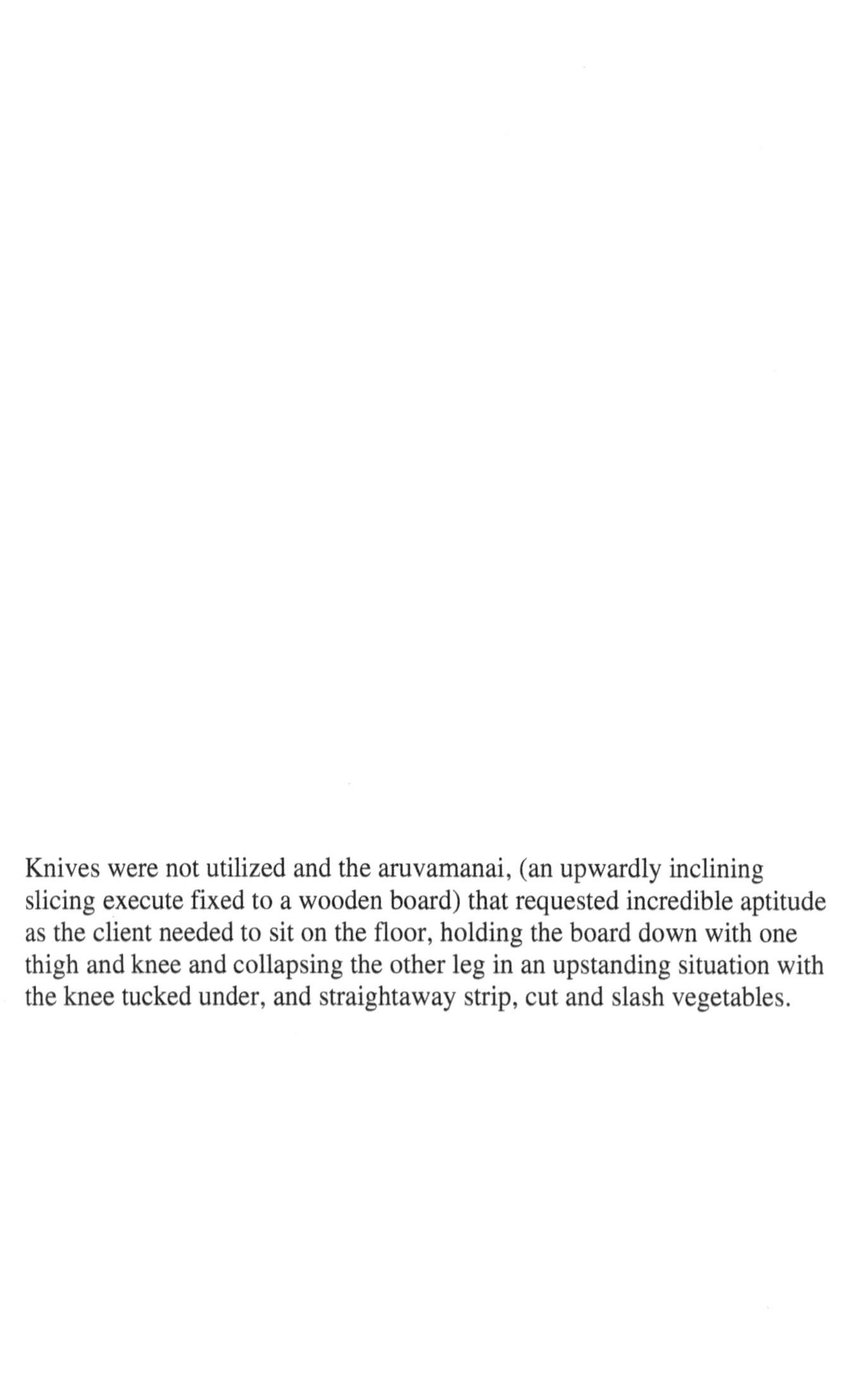

Knives were not utilized and the aruvamanai, (an upwardly inclining slicing execute fixed to a wooden board) that requested incredible aptitude as the client needed to sit on the floor, holding the board down with one thigh and knee and collapsing the other leg in an upstanding situation with the knee tucked under, and straightaway strip, cut and slash vegetables.

Every piece of the banana plant is valuable to the housewife and her home. It was filled in the lawn of each home, and was effectively accessible to all classes of individuals. That might have been the justification for why the ready banana was a significant element of pujas. The people of yore knew the moment restoration properties of the banana and the cerebrum supporting characteristics of potassium. So they made it a basic piece of Hindu life.

The various flavors assumed a significant part in the last allure of the dishes. Each fixing utilized in the Tamil food has a reason that goes beyond
taste and surface: fenugreek is a stomach related guide, cumin has numerous uses, dried vegetables and beans are nature's small cases of proteins, pepper is great for colds and hacks, turmeric mends wounds.

Growing, purchasing, cooking vegetables is a journey of disclosure. The people of yore knew it and the Tamil people group, knowledgeable in the Vedas, had soaked up and adjusted the legend of these people of yore into their day to day routines. The USP of this book is that it gives plans that were viewed as universal cooking. Onion and garlic don't include by any stretch of the imagination in the plans. The vegetables and organic products utilized in the plans are native or local produce.

You can go into the pages of this book and appreciate dealing with the plans that have been tried in large number of kitchens more than a few centuries. The easy to understand strategies and the fixings and hardware, accessible effectively in many homes, will cheer your hearts and fill your stomachs with great solid and scrumptious food.

The gift "Anna daatha, sukhibhava"/one who offers food stays blissful - says it all.

Note: The conventional chakki in Hindi and yendhram in tamil. The ammi (on the right above) is a flexible stone carry out. You could handle the surface of any glue that is ground on it. It is likewise a pressure buster, as girls in-regulation can take out their disappointments by moving the more modest stone piece with energy and a lot of commotion to enlist their quiet fights! This is valid as I encountered this myself. Amusing for sure. The ammi assumes a significant part in weddings and birth functions. It addresses the strong reinforcement of a conjugal relationship. A lady of the hour puts her foot on the stone processor while the husband slips the toe ring on her subsequent toe. The
endrum/chakki is likewise connected with thorough work, particularly in prison

disciplines. Rice was beat in a mortar or ground in the endhrum or chakki, a factory comprised of two level round rock sections with the top piece pivoted over the fixed base chunk. There was such a lot of merriment and straightforwardness during our youth that are really extraordinary. Life was loaded up with basic goodness, and we constantly wound up chuckling at hand crafted jokes now and then senseless yet sounded so great paying attention to our own giggling. I truly miss those times. Guiltlessness and straightforwardness was the characteristic of our childhood.

PLEASE READ OVER THESE.

IMPORTANT TIPS ON

INGREDIENTS

TAMARIND: Prepare a puree of the tamarind/ imli by soaking a handful of it (200gms) in a cup of hot water for four hours. Remove as much of the fiber and seeds as you can. Now add a little more water and pressure-cook on medium high for a whistle. Open lid when the hissing subsides. Cool it down a little more. Remove some more remaining fibers and seeds. Now puree in a blender. Store in the refrigerator and use. This way the skin is not wasted and is wholly used in a dish. Never buy store bought tamarind purée ever. They are adulterated, and additives are used. Do have the patience to prepare from basics at home. And, do not dilute the pulp until required.

Use 1½ - 2 tablepoons of the glue for a sauce without lentils, similar to the vethal kuzhambu or 1 tablespoonful of glue for a sambar with vegetables and lentils. Assuming you lean toward less tartness utilize less of the tamarind purée.

ASAFETIDA: Many brands of asafetida/hing, in both lump and powder structures, are accessible available. There are various approaches to utilizing a square of gelled asafetida. To get a valid flavor, this piece can be attacked bits when it is delicate. Plan little balls and microwave for 30 seconds.

Open, turn the squares around and microwave for another 20-25 seconds. Cool, pound them in a mortar and pestle and powder in an espresso processor or a blender and use routinely. The subsequent strategy is to absorb each ball in turn a quarter cup of water. This broke up asafetida glue can be utilized more than a few days whenever put away in a fridge. On the off chance that a square becomes dry and hard, cut it with a nutcracker or pound it into bits with a sledge. Do watch out for your fingers! Gelled asafetida is desirable over the locally acquired powders, which has plain flour or wheat flour added to it and tastes really lighter. Please desist from buying the powder available in the market. They are sub optimal. I would recommend to blacklist them altogether.

MUSTARD SEEDS/Rai are utilized in Indian cooking for preparing. Heat a teaspoon of oil or ghee in a pan and add the mustard. Take care to close the top of the container as the seeds will more often than not jump out while popping and can cause gentle consumes. Mustard can be minuscule, yet its consume can be powerful awkward! Continuously add the remainder of the flavoring fixings as soon as

the mustard starts to pop. While the popping is practically done, add the remainder of the dish to complete.

SALT has been reasonably utilized in every one of the plans. Utilize somewhat more salt for the podis (powders) and the pickles. For different dishes, be reasonable in its utilization. Test in the underlying stages until you know the amount that suits your sense of taste. Continuously recollect that less salt is more straightforward to fix than more.

A note on salt

SEA SALT is created through dissipation of sea water or water from salt water lakes, as a rule with little handling. Contingent upon the water source, this leaves behind specific hints of minerals and components. The minerals add flavor and shading to the ocean salt, which additionally comes in different degrees of coarseness.

TABLE SALT is regularly mined from underground salt stores. Table salt is all the more vigorously handled to dispose of minerals and typically contains an added substance to forestall clustering. Most table salt is likewise treated with iodine, a fundamental supplement that keeps a sound thyroid. Ocean salt and table salt have a similar fundamental dietary benefit, notwithstanding the way that ocean salt is regularly advanced as being better. Ocean salt and table salt contain similar measures of sodium by weight. Whichever kind of salt you appreciate, do as such in moderation.

PRESSURE PAN: A tension container saves time and holds the shading and kind of the different fixings. Vegetables, *sambars*, *kuzhambus*, lentils and kootus might be arranged straightforwardly in pressure-dish, as additionally in profound pots or skillets.

1. GREEN VEGETABLES: Heat half a cup of water with salt in a pressure-pan. Add the chopped vegetables and toss them lightly with a ladle. You will notice the vegetables turning a rich green. Close the lid and cook for one whistle. Turn off the heat and place the pan under cold running water. Once all the steam has been released, remove the stopper and open the pan carefully. The vegetables, green and tender looking, are now ready to be used as specified in the recipe.

2. SAMBARS and KUZHAMBUS: Add every one of the flavors with the popped

mustard seeds, curry leaves, tamarind, water, salt and asafetida alongside the vegetables. Follow a similar strategy as nitty gritty for green vegetables, yet you really want not place the dish under cool running water. Permit the murmuring sound to stop prior to opening the lid.

3. DALS/PULSES (all lentils): Heat some water in an open skillet with a tablespoon of lemon juice (to keep the foundation of the dish from obscuring) until it comes to the bubble. For best outcomes, red gram should be washed well and absorbed boiling water for 15 minutes prior to cooking. Inside a couple of moments, the gram will twofold in size. Utilize a tension skillet or strain cooker to cook the gram. On the off chance that you really want delicate and pale consistency, concoct to 3 - 4 whistles. Switch off the hotness and permit the skillet to cool until the murmuring sound stops totally. Open the top and utilize the cooked gram as indicated in the recipe.

PIGEON PEAS: If in a tension dish, absorb the peas heated water for 15 minutes, adding a quarter teaspoon of turmeric. Cook in 2½ cups of water until they transform into a delicate mash.

RICE COOKER: This apparatus generally accompanies an internal dish; add 1½ to 2 cups of water to it and utilize a tablespoon of lemon-juice to forestall obscuring of the inward dish, except if it is non-stick product. Keep the rice in a different metallic dish and spot it in the rice cooker encompassed by water. The steamed rice is cushioned and better when cooked in a different dish. While cooking, open the cover of the cooker and mix two or multiple times with the goal that the food prepares evenly.

MICROWAVE: This is exceptionally advantageous. While setting up a colacassia broil or a potato cook in a microwave, at first penetrate the vegetable pieces with a fork, envelop them with a casement material and cook for three to four minutes. Strip the skin, cut into pieces, add the expected flavors and oil and meal the blend without shutting the cover of the dish. It gets simmered quicker in a microwave.

STORAGE: Refrigerate powders such as *sambar podi* and *pitlai podi,* coffee powder, flours (rice flour, bengal gram flour and plain flour) either in a zip- lock bag or in an airtight container. This assists with holding the flavor and newness for quite a while. Clear the wetness off of curry leaves, coriander leaves or mint leaves, delicately envelop by a kitchen paper, place in a zip-lock sack and store in the fridge. For greens and different fixings to remain fresh

for quite a while, guarantee no dampness gets into them.

COOKING TIME: has been referenced in the various phases of setting up the dish. Planning TIME as given is just cleaving the veggies, grinding the coconut and preparing the tamarind sauce. The PREP TIME and PORTIONS have consequently been referenced for each dish.

NOTE

This book is useful to the cook who opens the cooler, sees as a specific vegetable and needs a recipe.

The areas of this book depend on individual vegetables; each sub-segment subtleties an alternate formula for that one vegetable.

NOW HERE'S THE IMPORTANT POINT!

The plans are likewise recorded in the request in which they are served on a banana leaf or a plate at feast time, beginning from a yogurt pachadi/raita and happening to a dry sautéed food, a curry dish and a fundamental backup like a sambar or a kuzhambu and the resulting courses that are not shown here.

CLARIFIED BUTTER

ghee/ neiy

Ghee is a customary mode for singing food. Setting up an impressive tasting ghee is a craftsmanship. Basically, explained margarine/ghee is cooked a piece longer until it is brilliant and the milk solids at the base are toasted to a dull brown.

People with dairy awarenesses find ghee simple to process, as it is really a spread fat without the lactose. It is filled in as a garnish for white rice and sauce in South Indian menus. At our homes, ghee is never locally acquired. Ghee arranged at home with unsalted margarine is healthy and delightful. Dissimilar to different oils, ghee will set into a dull honey shaded semi-strong as it cools, particularly in chilly environments. It is critical to take note of that whenever eliminated when actually yellow, the taste isn't awesome and the ghee doesn't smell lovely for a really long time. Liquefy little amounts of the ghee to serve at whatever point required. The dark buildup can be transformed into a delicious nibble by blending in with a tablespoon of wheat flour and a tablespoon of brown sugar.

Method:

Place one lb of unsalted margarine in a weighty lined pan over moderate hotness. Whenever it melts and reaches boiling point, bring down the hotness and mix to accelerate the liquefying system. When completely softened, it begins to bubble; bring down the fire a bit. Guarantee the foaming is consistent, as the margarine can leap out of the skillet and shower onto the burner. Go on for a couple of more minutes until the milk protein isolates and you observe that there is a layer on the top and dull pieces at the lower part of the skillet. At the point when it is a dull honey in shading, right away eliminate from the fire and cool it for 15 minutes. Cautiously strain through a fine lattice sifter or through a cheddar material, guaranteeing the dark buildup stays in the sifter. Store the ghee at room temperature in a bricklayer container or a glass compartment with a firm lid.

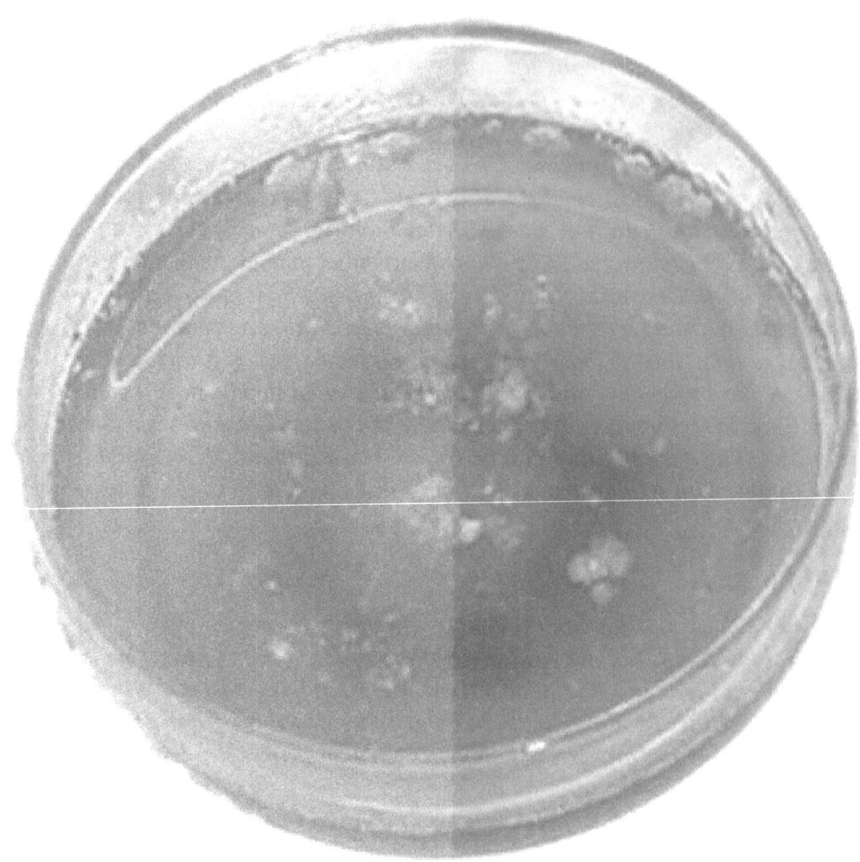

Timely tip: Unlike different oils, ghee will set into a yellow semi-strong as it cools, particularly in chilly environments. Try not to refrigerate; in the event that it is utilized routinely it stays new for very nearly a month.

ALL SPICE POWDER

sambar podi

Spice powders are significant taste enhancers in South Indian food. The plans are given over from one age to another and can have the unmistakable stamp of a specific district, local area or even only a family. In Tamil homes, the flavors are beat in a mortar or ground in a plant comprised of two level stone wheels All the fixings utilized for these powders are important for Ayurvedic consumes less calories. Set them up at home to partake in a sound and healthy lifestyle.

Ingredients:

3 cups coriander seeds

1 cup pigeon peas/thuvar dal

½ cup bengal gram/chana dal

1½ cups husked entire dark gram/urad dal

¼ cup fenugreek seeds

¼ cup mustard

seeds 2 tbsps

cumin seeds

½ cup dried red chillis

¼ cup peppercorns

½ cup curry leaves

8 long slender turmeric pieces or 3 tbsps turmeric powder

Method:

1. Wash and wipe the curry leaves dry.

2. Roast every one of the fixings in a pot over a medium fire for a few minutes until the lentils become light brilliant and begin producing their particular aromas.

3. Now add the curry leaves and mix for a 30 seconds.

4. Blend every one of the fixings into a fine powder. A few homes spread every one of the fixings out in the sun to dry the entire day, and afterward powder them.

5. Store in an impermeable holder. You can refrigerate it as well.

THE TASTE MAKER

pitlai podi

Ingredients:

3 cups coriander seeds

1 cup bengal gram/chana dal

¾ cup dried red chillis

5 marble-sized squares or 1½ tsps of asafetida/hing

powder 2 cups ground coconut

2 tsps oil

Method:

1. Heat a teaspoon of oil over medium hotness and dish the coriander seeds, bengal gram and red chillis until the lentil becomes golden.

2. Heat a large portion of a teaspoon oil and meal the asafetida blocks. Squash them into little pieces with a spatula so the internal parts are simmered also. Keep aside.

3. Heat the excess oil and meal the ground coconut until brilliant in color.

4. Blend every one of the fixings into a coarse powder.

5. Store in a jug and refrigerate to keep going a long time.

BOTTLE GOURD

soraikai/ doodhi/ lauki

Bottle gourd, bottle squash, and calabash gourd are scrumptious vegetables that can supplant debris gourd in plans. Bottle gourd has a sensitive nutty flavor and can be added to sauces and rice dishes. It can likewise be utilized to spread the word about sweet dishes.

ASH GOURD

pooshinikkai/ petha

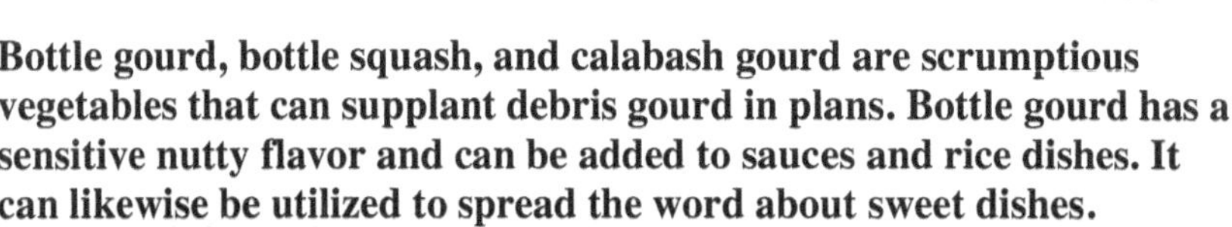

As kushmandam in Sanskrit, the debris pumpkin/debris gourd has extraordinary therapeutic worth. It is round or elongated in shape and has a fine covering on its skin like it has been moved in debris. This pasty wax outside prevents miniature creatures and gives the vegetable a long time span of usability. It tends to be put away for up to a year without refrigeration.

Known for its diuretic characteristics, the vegetable contains calcium, iodine and fluorine. The shoots, rings, and leaves of the plant may likewise be eaten as greens. An exceptionally adaptable vegetable, it is utilized to make fundamental dinner dishes and sweet dishes as well!

It is likewise used to eliminate

the hostile stare. PURCHASING

TIPS

a. Generally, the vegetable is bought in cut slices, as the full vegetable can be huge. Smaller varieties are now available, though.

b. Within should be white and firm.

c. Any staining means that it being rotten.

d. The seeds are a sign of the delicacy of the vegetable.

e. When it isn't new, it emanates an interesting smell so use it when you purchase it.

PREPARATION TIPS

a. Slice the vegetable and deseed it.

b. Carefully strip the external, waxy thick green skin and dispose of it.

c. Cut the vegetable into shapes or juliennes and cook.

d. Take care to utilize less salt and water when you cook, as the actual vegetable sheds heaps of water during the cooking process.

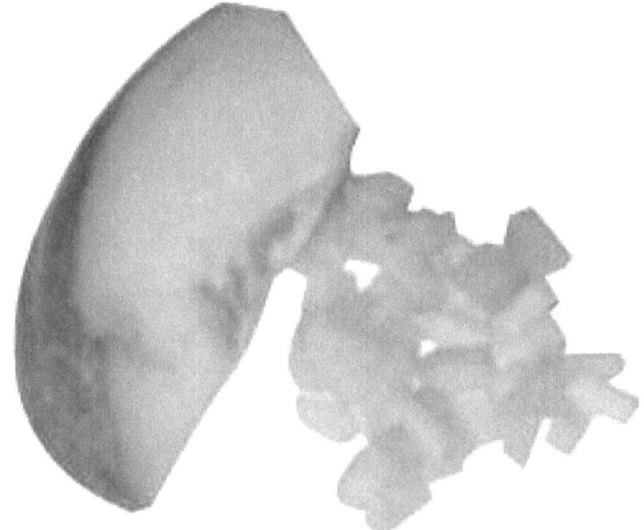

ASH GOURD STIR FRY

pooshini paruppu kari

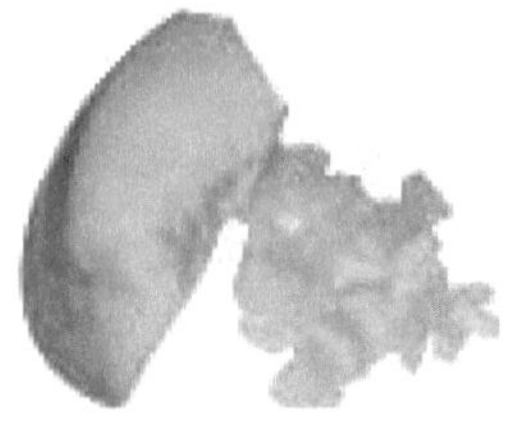

Prep Time: 12 mins. Serves 3 portions

An instantly prepared kari, it is fine textured and one that is full of healthy bites of a tender and soft vegetable.

Ash Gourd Stir Fry

Ingredients:

2 tsps split husked green gram/moong dal

½ lb debris gourd

¼ tsp asafetida/hing

powder 1 tsp sambar

powder

½ tsp

salt 2

tbsps

oil

For Seasoning:

¼ tsp mustard seeds

1 dried red stew, halved

½ tsp oil

Method:

1. Cover and absorb the green gram heated water for 20 minutes or until it fills in size.

2. Add salt to the water and cook the lentil for two minutes until delicate however firm. Keep aside.

3. Peel the toughness of the debris gourd totally, uncovering the white of the inside.

4. Discard the seed inside and cut the vegetable into little cubes.

5. Heat some water with salt and cook the vegetable for three minutes until delicate. Keep aside.

6. Heat oil in a pan, pop the mustard seeds and dish the red bean stew for five seconds. Add asafetida powder and sambar powder. Mix in the vegetable, green gram, squashed wet curry leaves and tenderly combine all as one. Really look at the salt substance and eliminate from fire.

7. Serve hot as a side or as a principle dish blended in with rice and ghee.

Important Note: Use various boiled vegetables like bottle gourd, green squash, yellow squash or even a medley of green vegetables to prepare this dish.

TANGY ASH GOURD CURRY

pooshini puli kuzhambu

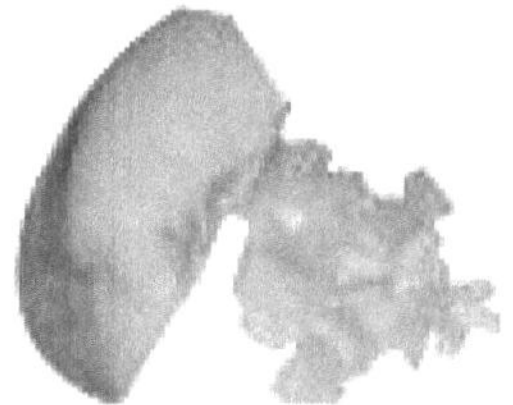

Prep Time: 12 mins. Serves 3 portions

A curry that is full of healthy bites of the soft vegetable with chunky brown chick peas.

Tangy Ash Gourd Curry

Ingredients:

¼ cup earthy colored chick peas

½ lb debris gourd

1 cup pigeon peas/thuvar dal

1 lime-sized tamarind lump, splashed and mash

separated A squeeze earthy colored sugar/jaggery

powder, optional

10 curry leaves

½ tsp

salt 2

tbsps

oil

For Seasoning:

¼ tsp mustard seeds

1 tsp split husked dark gram

¼ tsp asafetida/hing

powder 1 tsp oil

For The Paste:

¾ cup coconut,

ground 2 tbsps

coriander seeds 2

tbsps bengal gram

2 - 3 dried red chillis

Method:

1. Cover and absorb the earthy colored chickpea boiling water for 6 to 8 hours or until it fills in size.

2. Pressure-cook with pigeon peas for a whistle, lower fire and cook for 7-8 minutes. Switch off the fire and when the strain decreases totally, open and use.

3. Peel the toughness of the debris gourd totally and dispose of.
Cut the vegetable into cubes.

4. Heat a large portion of a teaspoon of oil and brown the bengal gram, coriander seeds and red chillis in a specific order. Keep aside.

5. Now add the ground coconut and somewhat brown. Grind all to a fine glue in a blender, adding a large portion of some water.

6. Heat some water with salt and cook the vegetable for 5 to 7 minutes until delicate. Add the cooked earthy colored chick peas, lentil, tamarind remove and mixed glue and bubble for five minutes.

7. Heat oil in a pot, pop the mustard seeds and brown the dark gram.
Add the asafetida powder to this, mix and add to the gravy.

8. Add a touch of jaggery or earthy colored sugar to adjust the flavors.
Add wet and squashed curry leaves and mix. Fill in as a primary course.

Tasty Tip: Use various boiled vegetables like bottle gourd, green squash, yellow squash or even a mixture of vegetables to the chick peas. You can add two tablespoons of the pitlai powder, roast a tablespoon of fresh grated coconut and add to the curry, or you can also add coconut milk to save yourself the trouble. Each of these steps will give a different flavor to the basic curry.

"Debris Gourd Coconut Gravy" and "Zesty Ash Gourd Curry" are found in my book, 'Samayal' in the Vegetable Stews and Curries segment.

BITTER GOURD

paharkai/ karela

The unpleasant gourd has astounding therapeutic excellencies. It is a cure for poison and an antipyretic to control fever. It fills in as a starter, is great for stomach throbs and bile and goes about as a laxative.

Bitter gourd is explicitly utilized in local medication for diabetes, heaps, clogging, blood and respiratory issues and cholera control.

BUYING TIPS

a. There are two assortments accessible a dim green one and a light green one.

b. The vegetable should be flexible when twisted.

c. Avoid purchasing assuming there are indications of yellowing or orange streaks outwardly, it implies that the vegetable has started to mature. When ready, it is more earnestly to cook.

d. The vegetable should be light, as that is an indication that the seeds inside have not started to ripen.

PREPARATION TIPS

a. Wash, top and tail the vegetable.

b. Slice into two halves.

c. Deseed the internal parts and afterward slash into the required size.

d. Sometimes the seeds are delicate. You might utilize them.

STIR FRIED BITTER GOURD IN YOGURT

paharkai thayir pachadi

Prep Time: 8 mins. Serves 3 portions

A traditional vegetable dish made in an unusual style.

Stir Fried Bitter Gourd in Yogurt

Ingredients:

2 medium-sized unpleasant gourds

A squeeze cayenne pepper/bean

stew powder 2 cups yogurt, beaten

¼ tsp mustard

seeds 3 tbsps oil

¼ tsp salt

Method:

1. Chop the severe gourd into flimsy roundabout or semi-round pieces.

2. Heat 2½ teaspoons of oil in a non-stick dish and sauté the vegetable and bean stew powder over medium hotness for 5 - 7 minutes until it becomes brown and crispy.

3. Heat a large portion of a teaspoon of oil and pop the mustard.

4. Add the mixed vegetable, salt, popped mustard to the yogurt and blend well. Alternatively, you can keep away from the popped mustard.

BITTER GOURD GREEN KARI

paharkai pachai kari

Prep Time: 10 mins. Serves 4 portions

A simple dish that can be made in a matter of minutes.

Bitter Gourd Green Kari

Ingredients:

2 medium severe gourds

½ tsp sugar or earthy

colored sugar 2 tbsps

coconut, grated

½ tsp salt

¼ tsp mustard seeds

½ tsp husked split dark gram/urad dal

½ tsp oil

Method:

1. Trim the finishes of the harsh gourd, cut longwise and cut into little pieces or cleave into wanted shape.

2. Heat a large portion of some water in skillet and add the vegetable with salt. Close the cover and cook for 3 - 4 minutes over a medium flame.

3. Open the top and let the water dissipate. Put away. On the other hand, destroy in the microwave for a few minutes. Remove.

4. Heat the oil, pop the mustard and brown the dark gram. Add the vegetable and brown sugar.

5. Take off the fire and blend the coconut.

6. Serve fresh.

BITTER GOURD IN CRUMBLED LENTIL

paharkai usili

Prep Time: 10 mins. Serves 3 portions

An unusual tasting vegetable crumble: prepare it and enjoy its native taste.

Bitter Gourd in Crumbled Lentil

Ingredients:

1 lb severe gourd

¼ tsp turmeric powder

½ tsp brown sugar

½ tsp salt

For The Usili:

1 cup pigeon peas/thuvar dal

4 or 5 dried red chillis

½ tsp asafetida/hing powder

¼ tsp turmeric powder

½ tsp salt

1. Dissolve the gram in steaming hot water for 15 minutes.

2. Blend coarsely with chillis, asafetida, turmeric and salt for the usili.

3. Steam for around 10 minutes in a rice cooker or level the usili and zap in the microwave for 2 - 3 minutes.

4. When an embedded wooden pick/fork tells the truth, the usili is done.

5. Cool the steamed lentil and disintegrate without lumps.

For Seasoning:

¼ tsp mustard

seeds 12 - 14

curry leaves

½ cup sesame oil

Method:

1. Trim closures, de-seed and quarter the vegetable.

2. Heat ½ cup of water in a profound dish with salt and add the hacked vegetable. Throw delicately with a spatula until rich green in color.

3. Over a medium fire, cover and cook for two minutes. Open and sauté until delicate yet firm. Keep aside.

4. Heat the oil and pop the mustard. Add the usili combination and mix well for three minutes. Set aside.

5. Add the vegetable, delicately mix for two minutes over medium hotness and add the earthy colored sugar. Add more salt whenever required. Add wet squashed curry leaves,

mix briefly until delicate and crumbly.

6. Serve with a primary course meal.

BITTER GOURD LENTIL SAUCE

paharkai sambar

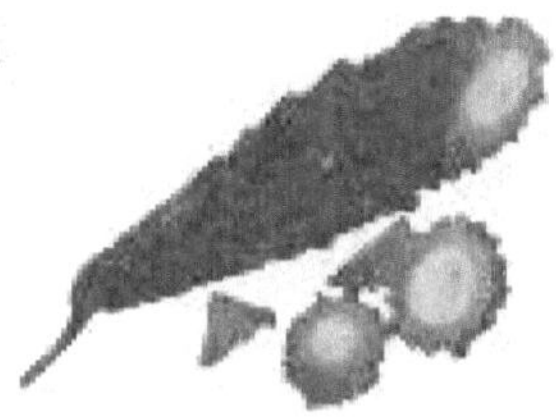

Prep Time: 10 mins. Serves 3 portions

The canny housewife would cook the bitter gourd and camouflage it into a tasty sweet and sour sauce that was good for her family's health. The authentic "Bitter Gourd Tangy Sauce" recipe is available in my book

'Samayal'.

Ingredients:

½ cup pigeon peas/thuvar dal

2 medium unpleasant gourd

1½ tsps thick tamarind purée

¼ tsp turmeric

powder 1½ tbsps

sambar powder

½ tsp asafetida

powder 10 curry

leaves

½ tsp jaggery/molasses

½ tsp salt

For Seasoning:

¼ tsp mustard seeds

½ tsp fenugreek

seeds 2 tsps oil

Method:

1. Cook the pigeon peas in 2½ cups of water to an extremely delicate consistency. Then again, pressure cook for a whistle, bring down the fire and cook for 3-4 minutes.

2. Switch off the fire and when the strain diminishes totally, open and use.

3. Slice the harsh gourd into half moons or quarter them.

4. Heat the oil, pop the mustard and brown the fenugreek. Add the cleaved vegetable and sauté for two minutes. Add turmeric powder, asafetida powder, salt and 1½ cups of water. Stew over a medium fire for 12 minutes or until the vegetable is soft.

5. Stir in the tamarind mash and stew for a couple more minutes. Add the *sambar powder, jaggery and cooked pigeon peas.*

6. Stir for several minutes. Add wet squashed curry leaves and mix again.

Tasty Tip: Palghat chefs deep fry the bitter gourd and add the vegetable after the gravy is cooked. They also roast a tablespoon of grated coconut until brown and the aroma is released. This is added finally as a garnish.

BROAD BEANS

avarakkai/ papdi

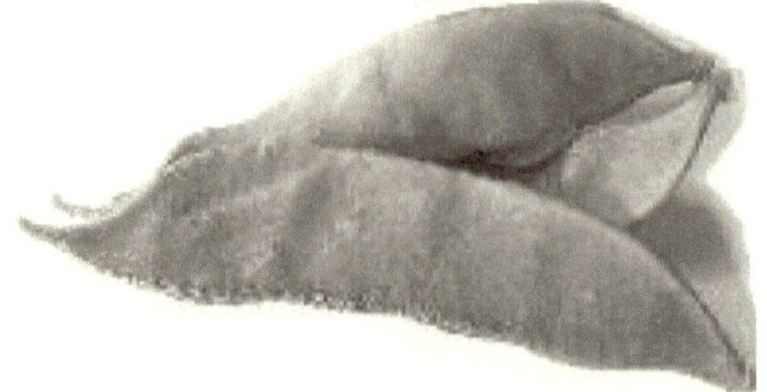

Indian wide beans are likewise called lilva beans or lablab beans. It is an all level bean, a more extensive form of the french beans. It is now and again alluded to as "yaanai kadhu kaai" (elephant-ears vegetable) in Tamil. At the point when the vegetable gets riper, the seeds are stout and somewhat sweet and high in protein. The vegetable is wealthy in iron too and gives high fiber content. It is critical to take note of that local green vegetables when cooked must be delicate to

nibble, not crunchy.

BUYING TIPS

a. The bean should be a rich green in color.

b. The bean should be level and the seeds should not project on the skin.

Preparation tips

a. Carefully take out the string on the two sides of the vegetable as you top and tail them.

b. Wash in running water and drain.

c. Cut into equal parts or three pieces, or hack them fine.

d. Use the seeds in a similar dish or independent and cook in any sauce dish.

BROAD BEANS IN CRUMBLED LENTILS

avarekai usili

Prep Time: 8 mins. Serves 3 portions

The vegetable gives a unique taste to this high protein dish.

Broad Beans in Crumbled Lentils

Ingredients:

1lb wide beans

¼ tsp turmeric powder

½ tsp salt

For The Usili:

½ cup pigeon peas/thuvar dal

7 dried red chillis

¼ tsp asafetida powder

½ tsp salt

Method:

1. Cover the gram in steaming hot water for 15 - 20 minutes.

2. Blend coarsely with chillis, asafetida, turmeric and salt for the usili.

3. Steam for around 20 minutes until cooked or level the usili hitter and zap in the microwave for 2 - 3 minutes. Eliminate when you can embed a wooden pick or fork and it comes out clean.

4. Cool the steamed lentils and disintegrate without irregularities by grinding or mixing utilizing the beat mode.

For Seasoning:

¼ tsp mustard

seeds 12 - 14

curry leaves

½ cup sesame oil

Method:

1. Trim closures and cleave the vegetable fine.

2. Heat some water in a profound container, adding salt.

3. When it bubbles, add the vegetable and mix until wealthy in shading. Close cover somewhat and lower fire to medium. Cook for 3 - 4 minutes until delicate to the touch. Keep aside.

4. If the water is in overabundance, save to the side and use for another gravy.

5. Heat the oil, pop the mustard; add the usili and mix for a few minutes. Change zest levels, mix again and add the vegetable. Add wet squashed curry leaves, blend generally well and serve new for a principle course meal.

BROAD BEANS SPICY STIR FRY

avarekai urapu kari

Prep Time: 8-10 mins. Serves 2 portions

A spicy kari bursting with delightful mild flavors.

Broad Beans Spicy Stir Fry

Ingredients:

½ lb wide
beans 3 curry
leaves
½ tsp salt
Roast And
Powder: 1 tsp
coriander seeds
1 tbsp bengal
gram 2 dried red
chillis
½ tsp oil

Method:

Heat oil to broil the bengal gram, the coriander seeds and the dried red chilies in a specific order. At the point when the smells consume the atmosphere eliminate from fire. Powder coarsely and keep aside.

For Seasoning:

¼ tsp mustard seeds

½ tsp split husked dark gram/urad dal

¼ tsp asafetida/hing

powder 1 tsp oil

Method:

1. Trim closures and slash the vegetable fine.

2. Heat some water in a profound dish, adding salt. Whenever it bubbles, add the vegetable and mix until wealthy in shading. Close cover to some degree and lower fire to medium. Cook for 3-4 minutes until delicate to the touch. Eliminate from flame.

3. If the water is in abundance, save to the side and use for another gravy.

4. Heat the oil, pop the mustard, add the dark gram to brown daintily, and add the asafetida. Presently add the expansive beans and powdered flavors and sauté briefly. Add wet squashed curry leaves, mix for 30 seconds and remove.

5. Serve as a delectable side dish for a primary course with steamed rice.

TASTY BROAD BEANS CURRY

avarekai kootu

Prep Time: 12 mins. Serves 3 portions

The fragrance of cooked beans and green gram in spices adds in loads of yummy factor to the dish.

Tasty Broad Beans Curry

Ingredients:

¼ cup husked split green gram/moong dal

¼ kilo expansive beans, chopped

½ tsp salt

For The Paste:

1 dried red chilli

2 tbsps ground coconut

½ tsp asafetida/hing powder

1 tbsp husked split dark gram/urad dal

For Seasoning:

¼ tsp mustard seeds

½ tsp husked split dark gram/urad dal

10 curry

leaves 1½

tsps oil

Method:

1. Wash, top and tail and hack the vegetable fine.

2. Heat a teaspoon of oil, broil the red stew, add asafetida powder and dark gram and daintily brown them.

3. Blend with coconut into a coarse paste.

4. Cook the green gram in some water until delicate. Then again, pressure cook for a whistle, lower fire and cook for 2-3 minutes. At the point when the tension decreases totally, eliminate top and use.

5. In a profound container, add some water and salt. Cook the slashed vegetable until delicate. Add the mixed glue and green gram, mix delicately and let it bubble for two minutes. Thicken and eliminate from flame.

6. In a little container, heat the leftover oil, pop the mustard and brown the dark gram. Add this to the sauce. Add all together and mix for two or three minutes or until the sauce thickens marginally. Wet and pound the curry leaves and add to the stewing gravy.

Tasty Tip: Add a tablespoon of raw coconut oil to the kootu after you remove it from the stove. The flavor is exotic. You can also add store-bought coconut milk or dry coconut powder available in Indian and Thai grocery stores.

SPICY BROAD BEANS GRAVY

avarekai poritha kootu

Prep Time: 12 mins. Serves 3 portions

This dish is a huge favorite in Tamil homes. It tastes fabulous when served with steamed rice with a dollop of cooked yellow split peas and a few drops of ghee.

Spicy Broad Beans Gravy

Ingredients:

½ cup pigeon peas/thuvar dal

1 lb wide beans

¼ tsp turmeric powder

½ tsp salt

For The Paste:

4 tbsps ground

coconut 1 dried red

chilli

4 peppercorns

¼ tsp asafetida/hing

powder 1 tbsp cumin

seeds

For Seasoning:

¼ tsp mustard seeds

¼ tsp husked split dark gram/urad dal

6 curry

leaves 1½

tsps oil

Method:

1. Soak pigeon peas in steaming hot water for 15 to 20 minutes. Cook until soft.

2. Top and tail the vegetable and hack into meager bits.

3. Fry the stew in oil for seven seconds until it turns firm and radiant red. Add peppercorns, asafetida and toast for six seconds. Mix all with the cumin and coconut into a coarse glue. Keep aside.

4. Boil some water and salt in a profound container. Add the vegetable and cook over a medium fire for 5-6 minutes until delicate. Add the mixed glue and cooked lentil, mix tenderly to stew over a medium flame.

5. Heat the leftover oil, pop the mustard and brown the dark gram. Add to the poritha kootu and mix for two or three minutes until the sauce thickens marginally. Press wet curry leaves, add and mix for five seconds.

6. Serve this superb tasting dish as a principle course with steamed rice.

BROAD BEANS LENTIL CURRY

avarekai sambar

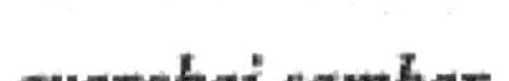

Prep Time: 6 mins. Serves 3 portions

The versatile sambar can be made with any vegetable.

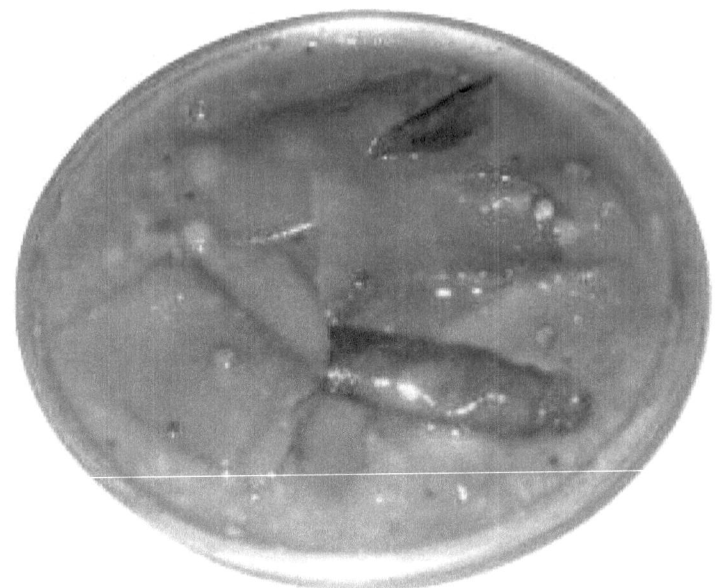

Broad Beans Lentil Curry

Ingredients:

½ cup pigeon peas/thuvar dal

2 tsps tamarind sauce

½ lb wide beans

¼ tsp asafetida/hing

powder 1½ tsps sambar

powder

10 curry leaves

½ bundle coriander leaves, optional

½ tsp salt

For Seasoning:

¼ tsp mustard seeds

¼ tsp fenugreek

seeds 1 tsp oil

Method:

1. Trim finishes and split the vegetable.

2. Soak the pigeon peas in steaming hot water for 15 minutes and cook in 2½ cups of water to a squash. Then again, pressure cook for a whistle, lower fire and cook for 10 minutes. At the point when the whistle lessens, totally open and use.

3. Heat the oil, pop the mustard and daintily brown the fenugreek seeds. Add the vegetable and sauté briefly. Add sambar powder, asafetida and some water. Cover and stew over a medium fire for 10 minutes until delicate. Add the tamarind sauce and salt. Cook for two or three minutes. Add the cooked lentil. At the point when it thickens marginally, add wet squashed curry leaves. Mix for 30 seconds and topping with finely cleaved coriander leaves.

CLUSTER BEANS

kothaverakai/ gavar ke phali

This green bean has a slightly bitter flavor and is a great source of fiber in diets. A young, fresh cluster bean pod is narrow and long. It is a native Indian vegetable. Young beans are retained as vegetables. The seeds of matured beans are harvested and crushed into flour. Known as guar gum, this flour becomes a gel in water. It is used in dairy products like ice cream and as a stabilizer in cheese and cold meat processing. Cluster beans are low in calories and help to lower blood sugar and cholesterol levels.

This vegetable is famously surrendered as a repentance when individuals visit Kasi (Benares). Subsequently, assuming that you are cooking for more established individuals, check assuming they eat this vegetable prior to remembering it for the menu. Please note and remember that native green vegetables have to be cooked till tender, they should not be crunchy.

BUYING TIPS

a. The beans must be tender and pliable and a rich green in color. The fresh ones have gloss.

b. If the beans are rough, then, at that point, they are not delicate and have begun ripening.

PREPARATION TIPS

a. Even the delicate and new group beans must be beaten and followed and require stringing.

b. Trim the finish of a bunch bean unit with your fingers, and afterward pull descending. In the event that a stringy string leaves away, the beans need stringing.

c. Repeat on the other side.

d. Slice the beans into gram measured pieces or cut into equal parts around one-inch length.

CLUSTER BEANS STIR FRY

kothaverakai kari

Prep Time: 10 mins. Serves 3 portions

A distinctively flavored vegetable, it tastes good plain or with powdered spices.

Cluster Beans Stir Fry

Ingredients:

1 lb bunch beans

¼ tsp asafetida/hing powder

½ tsp stew powder/cayenne

pepper 8 curry leaves

½ tsp

salt 4

tbsps

oil

For Seasoning:

¼ tsp mustard seeds

½ tsp husked split dark gram/urad dal

1 tsp oil

Method:

1. Top and tail to de-string the two sides of the group beans. Hack finely.

2. Heat the oil, pop the mustard seeds and brown the gram. Add a large portion of some water, salt the hacked vegetable and cook for 3 - 4 minutes until parboiled.

3. Let the water dissipate and afterward add asafetida powder, bean stew powder and the squashed curry leaves. Sauté for 20 to 30 seconds.

4. Remove from fire and serve new as a side dish with steamed rice and a primary course.

TANGY CLUSTER BEANS CURRY

kothaverakai puli kootu

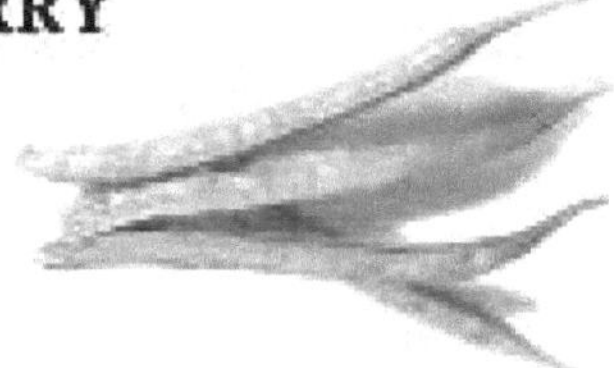

Prep Time: 10 mins. Serves 3 portions

This is a traditional favorite dish in my mother-in-law's home. It is a great tasting dish and we make it quite often. The brown sugar takes away the slight bitterness of the vegetable.

Tangy Cluster Beans Curry

Ingredients:

½ lb group beans

1 tbsp tamarind

purée 1 tsp sambar

powder

¼ tsp turmeric powder

½ tsp asafetida/hing

powder 8 curry leaves

1 tsp rice flour

½ tsp earthy

colored sugar 1

tsp salt

2 cups water

For The Seasoning:

¼ tsp mustard seeds

½ tsp bengal gram/chana dal

1 tbsp oil

Method:

1. Top, tail and string the two sides of the vegetable and slash fine.

2. Heat a large portion of some water in a non-stick skillet and cook the vegetable, adding a large portion of a teaspoon of salt, for 7 - 8 minutes until delicate and cooked. On the other hand, cook straightforwardly in a tension prospect whistle. Switch off and keep aside.

3. Heat oil, pop the mustard seeds and brown the gram. Add some water, blending in the tamarind puree, *sambar powder*, turmeric powder, asafetida powder, and a large portion of a teaspoon of salt. Close top and cook over a medium fire for 3 - 4 minutes. Open top and add the cooked vegetable with the water and mix for another 2 - 3 minutes until the curry is thick. Add the rice flour, wet and squashed curry leaves and earthy colored sugar. Mix for 30 seconds and eliminate from flame.

4. Add the rice flour, wet and squashed curry leaves and earthy colored sugar. Mix for 30 seconds and eliminate from flame.

CLUSTER BEANS IN CRUMBLED LENTILS

kothaverakai usili

Prep Time: 10 mins. Serves 4 portions

A favorite dish for traditional food lovers.

Cluster Beans in Crumbled Lentils

Ingredients:

½ lb bunch beans

10 curry leaves

½ tsp salt

For The Crumble:

1 cup pigeon peas/thuvar dal

3 - 4 dried red chillis

½ tsp asafetida/hing

powder 8 curry leaves

½ tsp salt

Method:

1. Cover the lentil in steaming hot water and splash for around 10 minutes. Mix coarsely alongside different elements for the crumble.

2. Steam for 15 minutes in a rice cooker or straighten the usili and zap in a microwave for 2-3 minutes. Embed a wooden pick/fork and when it tells the truth, the usili is done.

3. Cool the steamed lentil and disintegrate without bumps by grinding it or mixing utilizing beat speed.

For Seasoning:

½ tsp mustard

seeds 2 tsps

sesame oil

Method:

1. Heat the oil, pop the mustard. Add the usili blend and mix well for three minutes. Set aside.

2. Top and tail, string and cut the vegetables very fine.

3. Boil a large portion of some water with salt in a profound dish. Add the vegetable and cook for three to four minutes until done, or when the vegetable turns delicate and firm.

4. In another container, heat the oil and pop the mustard seeds. Add the lentil disintegrate and mix briefly prior to adding the vegetable. Mix this delicately over a medium fire for two minutes until delicate and brittle. Presently add wet squashed curry leaves, mix and remove.

DRUMSTICK

This stick-shaped vegetable grows on a tree and has a hard, green outer covering that gives it its name. Both pods and leaves can be eaten. There is an art to eating this vegetable, as only the soft, almost jelly-like interior, in which the seeds are embedded, is edible. The seeds are eaten when tender but never the outer skin, which is discarded after scooping out the pulp. The best way to eat a drumstick is to pick it up with the fingers and scrape the soft center

with the teeth. The woody exterior can also be chewed to extract the juices, both inherent and from the dish in which it is cooked, and then discarded on the side of the plate. Drumstick leaves have a wonderful flavor. The vegetable has medicinal value and is very high in iron content. It is good for high blood pressure.

BUYING TIPS

a. The drumstick should have a smooth, greenish skin.

b. Most drumsticks have slight knocks showing where the seeds are in the stick. Notwithstanding, stay away from those with articulated knocks and dainty spaces in between.

c. There should be negligible obstruction when the drumstick is turned, showing its tenderness.

d. Keep drumsticks enclosed by paper in the crisper cabinet of the fridge for a little while, however consume them early.

e. The most ideal way to keep them new for somewhat longer is to cleave them into 2 or 3 pieces, wrap and refrigerate.

PREPARATION TIPS

a. Wash the drumsticks and scratch off dry looking patches. Cut into finger length pieces and bubble them in adequate liquid.

b. Leave the leaves enveloped by a paper for the time being and they will get disconnected from the branches. In any case, culling them off the stems is a monotonous process.

c. There is no compelling reason to slash the leaves, as they are tiny.

d. Leaves should be washed in cool water and depleted in a colander.

SPICY DRUMSTICK CURRY

murungakai sambar

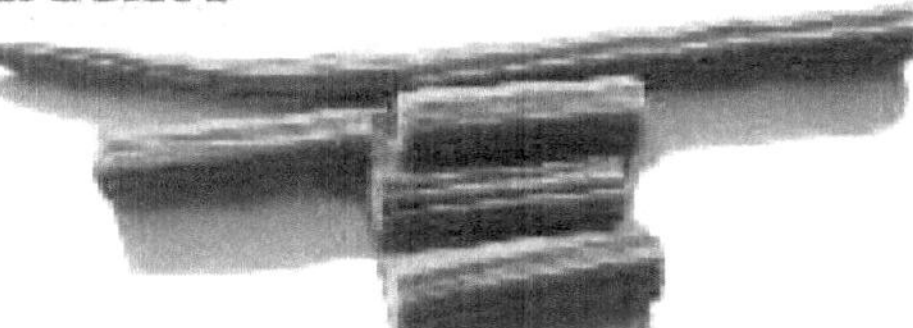

Prep Time: 8 mins. Serves 4 portions

Drumsticks from the backyard were freshly plucked off the tree and made into a variety of dishes, like this one.

Ingredients:

½ cup pigeon peas/thuvar dal

2 drumsticks, slashed into three-inch

pieces 1½ tsps tamarind sauce

¼ tsp asafetida/hing

powder 1½ tsps sambar

powder

8 curry leaves

A couple of twigs of cilantro, cleaved fine

½ tsp salt

For Seasoning:

¼ tsp mustard seeds

½ tsp fenugreek

seeds 1 tsp oil

Method:

1. Cook the lentil in two cups of water over medium hotness until soft. Then again, pressure cook for a whistle and lower fire to cook for 10 minutes. Whenever the tension diminishes totally, open and use.

2. In a profound skillet, add some water, hacked drumsticks, sambar powder and salt and cook over a medium fire for 8 - 10 minutes. Assuming the drumstick is overcooked, it will deteriorate; the external skin that is unpalatable can be irritating

and get stuck while gulping. Add the tamarind sauce and asafetida powder and mix tenderly for a few minutes.

3. Heat the oil, pop the mustard, daintily brown the fenugreek and add to the sauce. Add the cooked lentil and bubble over a medium fire for 3 - 4 minutes or until the sauce thickens. Mix in wet and squashed curry leaves and remove.

Healthy Tip: It is said that regular intake of drumsticks and okra boosts mental abilities. You can stir fry washed and cut fenugreek leaves and add to this sauce.

DRUMSTICK TANGY SAUCE

murungakai vathal kuzhambu

Prep Time: 6 mins. Serves 4 portions

This curry is always served with steamed rice, with a spoon of cooked pigeon peas and a dollop of melted ghee.

Drumstick Tangy Sauce

Ingredients:

2 slashed drumsticks hacked into three-inch pieces

3 tbsps tamarind sauce

½ tsp asafetida/hing

powder 1½ tbsps sambar

powder

8 curry leaves

2 tbsps sesame oil

¾ tsp salt

For Seasoning:

¼ tsp mustard seeds

1 dried red bean stew, halved

¼ tsp fenugreek seeds

Method:

1. Heat a teaspoon of oil, pop the mustard and softly brown the crisp and fenugreek. Add the hacked drumstick and mix for a large portion of a moment. Cover and stew for 8-10 minutes until the vegetable is cooked and delicate in within yet stays whole.

2. Stir in the tamarind sauce, some water, asafetida powder, sambar powder, and salt. Eliminate the top and thicken the kuzhambu. Add wet squashed curry leaves and with the excess sesame oil. Switch off the flame.

Timely Tip: Use this recipe and prepare any vathal kuzhambus with different vegetables like broad beans, okra, eggplant, etc. Save time by adding a teaspoon of rice flour or bengal gram flour in three tablespoons of water to thicken the gravy. The kuzhambu can be stored in the refrigerator and used for a few days.

EGGPLANT

kathirikai/ baingan

The eggplant (aubergine or brinjal) is firmly connected with the tomato and potato. It is native to southern India and Sri Lanka. At one time, it was accepted to be toxic. For the most part, eggplants are a protected vegetable to be eaten. They come in various shapes-a lengthened oval with a dim purple skin; a full dull purple assortment weighing as much as a kilogram; white to yellow or green eggplant; rosy purple or profound purple eggplant and a striped assortment. The crude vegetable becomes delicate when cooked. The sharpness of the vegetable can be eliminated by salting and washing the cut brinjal. Most current assortments needn't bother with this treatment, as they are less harsh. The brinjal can ingest a lot of cooking fats and sauces and result in very rich dishes. The salting system diminishes how much oil ingested. The vegetable will in general have loads of seeds that are palatable, alongside the slight skin. The brinjal need not be stripped. Research says that the eggplant/brinjal helps in the control and treatment of high blood cholesterol by achieve decreases of up to 30%. The vegetable is more extravagant in nicotine than some other palatable plant, however the sum is unimportant contrasted with detached smoking.

BUYING TIPS

a. When you purchase brinjals, the vegetable should be firm and smooth with a sparkling, immaculate skin. Pick little ones.

b. A smart thought is pick ones with new stalks.

c. Watch out for the little thistles around the stalks.

d. The more keen the thistles, the fresher the brinjals!

e. Allow a large portion of a pound of the vegetable for two people and a couple more
in the event you need to dispose of any.

f. The brinjal can be cooked without help from anyone else or alongside an assortment of other vegetables.

PREPARATION TIPS

a. Slice the brinjals as indicated in the recipe.

b. Sprinkle the cuts with salt and put them into a colander.

c. This will eliminate any bitterness.

d. Rinse and dry the cuts before using.

e. You can consume the skin off and cook just the pulp.

GRILLED EGGPLANT CHUTNEY

sutta kathirikai thuvayal

Prep Time: 5 mins. Serves 3 portions

The charred smokiness gives this chutney distinct flavor.

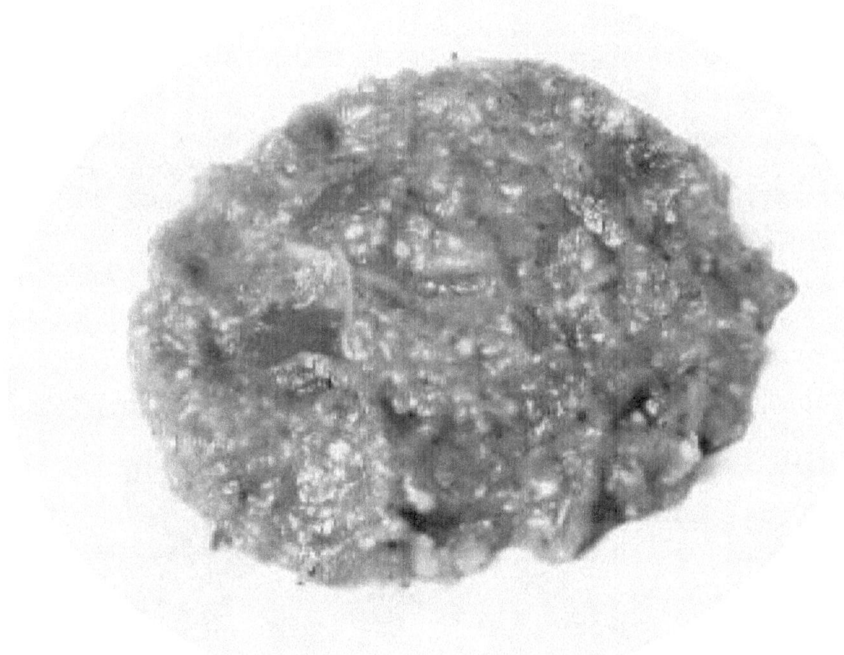

Grilled Eggplant Chutney

Ingredients:

1 large   eggplant

2 tsps husked split dark gram/urad dal

1½ tsps tamarind

glue 3 dried red

chillis

½ tsp salt

For The Seasoning:

¼ tsp mustard seeds

½ tsp husked split dark gram

½ tsp asafetida/hing

powder 1 tsp oil

Method:

1. Coat the eggplant with oil and meal uniformly on all sides straight over a high fire. Absorb water to cool; strip off the darkened skin and the tail neatly. Pound the mash and set aside.

2. Heat a teaspoon of oil, cook the red chillis and softly brown the gram. Eliminate from fire. Mix alongside tamarind and salt into a coarse glue to make a thick chutney. Add a little water provided that important, as the vegetable will turn soft. Blend into the mash and set aside.

3. Heat the excess oil, pop the mustard and gently brown the gram. Add the asafetida and mix for a second.

4. Remove from the fire and add to the chutney.

Tasty Tip: This dish makes an interesting dip or accompaniment to hors d'oeuvres.

MUSHY EGGPLANT BANANA KARI

katinja kari

Prep Time: 12 mins. Serves 3 portions

This dish takes its name from the packed food that was sent with the groom's party at weddings when they went back home the day after the ceremony. The meals, packed in banana leaves, were carried in a basket that is still called "kattu shathu mootai" or packed rice bundles. The menu was made up of mixed rice dishes and other finger food with some tangy veggies thrown in.

Mushy Eggplant Banana Kari

Ingredients:

1 green banana

½ lb eggplant

1½ tbsps tamarind purée

3 green chillis, cut lengthwise

¾ tsp asafetida/hing powder

¼ tsp turmeric

powder 8 curry

leaves

¾ tsp salt

1 cup water

For Seasoning:

¼ tsp mustard seeds

½ tsp husked split dark gram/urad dal

1 tsp oil

Method:

1. Peel and quarter the banana and absorb water to keep away from discoloration.

2. Cut the stem and cleave the eggplant into vertical pieces. Absorb the pieces one more dish of water to stay away from discoloration.

3. Heat some water. Add the banana pieces subsequent to depleting off the water. Add turmeric powder and cook on a medium fire for two minutes. Presently add the eggplant subsequent to depleting off the water. Cover and cook both for an additional two minutes until water is retained. At the point when the vegetables are cooked to delicateness, add the salt.

4. In another skillet, heat oil, pop the mustard seeds and brown the dark gram. Add the green chillis, vegetables, asafetida powder and finally, the tamarind purée. Stew for 40 seconds. Wet and pulverize the curry leaves and add. Mix briefly and add more salt if required.

5. Remove and fill in as a side dish.

SPICY STIR FRIED EGGPLANT

kathirikai roast

Prep Time: 10 mins. Serves 3 portions

Spicy brinjal prepared the South Indian way—a great delicacy.

Spicy Stir Fried Eggplant

Ingredients:

½lb eggplants

¼ tsp tamarind purée

¼ tsp turmeric powder

¼ tsp asafetida hing powder

¼ tsp bean stew powder

½ tsp salt

Oil for profound frying.

For Seasoning:

¼ tsp mustard seeds

¼ tsp oil

Method:

1. Chop the tail and cut upward into slight pieces. Absorb water.

2. Heat oil, channel the eggplant and fry five or six bits of the eggplant at a time. At the point when somewhat delicate and badly crumpled, eliminate and put in a plate fixed with paper towels to eliminate abundance oil.

3. Mix, turmeric powder, asafetida powder, bean stew powder and salt to the singed eggplant and mix in a dish over a low fire for 3-4 minutes until fresh and done.

4. Remove from fire and move to a serving bowl.

EGGPLANT RICE

vangi bath

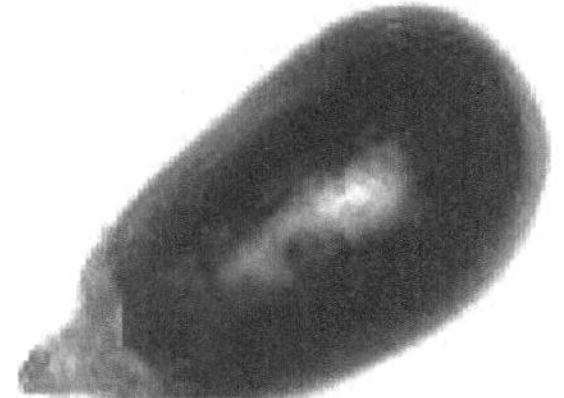

Prep Time: 10 mins. Serves 3 portions

Introduced by the Marathas when they ruled from Tanjore, vangi is the Marathi word for eggplant.

Eggplant Rice

Ingredients:

1 cup rice

1 tsp tamarind Juice, thinned

1 lb eggplant, cubed

¼ tsp turmeric

powder 1½ tbsps

pitlai powder 1tsp

salt

For Seasoning:

¼ tsp mustard

seeds 1 green

bean stew, slit

1 tbsp explained spread/ghee

10 curry leaves

4 tbsps oil

Method:

1. Cook the rice in 2½ cups of water until each grain is cushy. Put away to cool.

2. Heat the oil and pop the mustard, add the green bean stew and mix for five seconds. Add the slashed eggplant and turmeric powder. Mix well, cover and stew over a medium fire for five minutes. Open the top, mix and cook till the brinjal is delicate and done. Add tamarind juice, *pitlai powder and salt.* Cook for a couple more minutes.

3. Stir in the rice, curry leaves and ghee.

4. Remove from the flame.

Timely Tip: Medium or small-sized eggplant is available in Indian groceries. Zap the eggplant pieces, adding turmeric powder, in a microwave for 2-3 minutes. This will quicken the process.

LONG BEANS

karamani/ chowli bhaji

Long beans or "payathangai" are likewise referred to in the West as the since quite a while ago podded cowpea, asparagus bean, snake bean or Chinese long bean.

The beans are a decent wellspring of protein, nutrients An and C, thiamin, riboflavin, iron, phosphorus, potassium, magnesium and manganese.

BUYING TIPS

a. The vegetable should be a great green in shading and the seeds inside ought not shape bumps.

b. They should be thin and malleable and the vegetable ought not be yellow in color.

PREPARATION TIPS

a. Top and tail the vegetable and cut it into fine gram-sized pieces or into juliennes.

b. If the seeds project, split open the pods and de-seed.

c. Discard the skin, as it will be fibrous.

LONG BEANS COCONUT STIR FRY

karamani kari

Prep Time: 8 mins. Serves 3 portions

A dry stir fry easy to make, taking very little time.

Long Beans Coconut Stir Fry

Ingredients:

1 lb long beans

2 tbsps curry leaves

¼ tsp salt

For Seasoning:

¼ tsp mustard seeds

1 tsp husked split dark

gram 1 tsp oil

To Blend:

3 tbsps coconut, ground/frozen

½ cried red

stew 1 tsp

cumin seeds

Method:

1. Heat ½ teaspoon oil and dish the stew until red and fresh. Mix coarsely with coconut and cumin seeds, adding 1 to 2 teaspoons of water. Keep aside.

2. Trim finishes and cleave the vegetable into wanted shape.

3. Heat a large portion of some water in a profound dish with salt and add the vegetable. Throw delicately with a spatula until a rich green in color.

4. Over a medium fire, cover and cook for three minutes. Open and sauté until delicate yet firm. Keep aside.

5. Heat the leftover a large portion of a teaspoon of oil in a pot, pop the mustard seeds and brown the dark gram. Add wet and squashed curry leaves, long beans and the mixed glue. Mix over a medium fire for five seconds.

Tasty tip: To get an alternate flavor, you can sprinkle a little usili disintegrate. *Usili arrangement is given in the segment 'Group Beans in Crumbled Lentils' in the Cluster Beans chapter.*

LONG BEANS LENTIL CURRY

karamani kootu

Prep Time: 12 mins. Serves 3 portions

The lovely green of the beans and the yellow of the grams blend beautifully to make a curry that is as visually appealing as it is to the palate.

Long Beans Lentil Curry

Ingredients:

¼ cup husked split green gram/moong dal

½lb long beans, chopped

½ tsp salt

For the

paste

1 dried red chilli

¼ tsp asafetida/hing

powder 3 tbsps coconut,

grated

1 tbsp cumin seeds

For Seasoning:

¼ tsp mustard seeds

½ tsp husked split dark gram/urad dal

10 curry

leaves 1½

tbsps oil

Method:

1. Heat a teaspoon of oil and dish the red stew, mix in the asafetida powder. Presently gently brown the dark gram. Mix with coconut, cumin seed into a coarse paste.

2. Cook the green gram in some water until delicate. On the other hand, pressure-cook for a whistle, lower fire and cook for 2 - 3 minutes. Whenever the strain lessens totally, open cover and use.

3. In a profound container, add some water with salt and cook the vegetable until delicate. Add the mixed glue and cooked green gram, mix delicately and let it bubble for two minutes.

4. In another container, heat the leftover oil, pop the mustard and brown the split dark gram. Add this to the curry and mix for two or three minutes or until the sauce thickens somewhat. Wet and smash the curry leaves and add to the stewing gravy.

Tasty Tip: Add a dash (a tablespoon) of raw coconut oil to the kootu after you remove it from the stove. The flavor is exotic. You can also add coconut milk from a tetra pack, or dry powder available in Indian and Thai grocery stores.

OKRA

vendakkai/ bhindi

Okra, otherwise called woman's fingers in India, was acquainted with

the West by the Arabs in the twelfth or thirteenth century. Okra was brought into the USA by African slaves. The word is gotten from the West African word nkruma. In the East, it is known as woman's fingers on account of its shape. It is a long, slim green case with a somewhat fluffy skin and is brimming with palatable white seeds.

It is broadly filled in tropical and mild environments and has a place with the hibiscus and cotton plant family.

BUYING TIPS

a. Choose stems that snap neatly in the sharp end and don't bend.

b. It can be made into a dry dish or added to curries or blended vegetable dishes.

PREPARATION TIPS

a. Okra can be cooked entire, divided, hacked into adjusts or stuffed and grilled.

b. Wash the vegetable completely in the wake of absorbing it water.

c. Drain in a colander and afterward top and tail it.

d. The vegetable deliveries a glutinous sap when it is cooked.

e. So add a spoonful of curds or tamarind juice when you cook it.

f. Cook it in a griddle or wok, ideally non-stick.

g. Cover at first for three minutes and afterward keep on simmering it without a

top as the vegetable will go mushy.

h. To hold newness, cook inside three days of buying.

STIR FRIED OKRA IN YOGURT

vendakkai thayir pachadi

Prep Time: 5 mins. Serves 3 portions

A raita with stir fried okra—cool and crispy!

Stir Fried Okra in Yogurt

Ingredients:

½ lb okra

2 cups yogurt, beaten

¼ tsp mustard seeds

2 tsps oil

¼ tsp salt

Method:

1. Wash, wipe the vegetable and cleave into fine rounds.

2. Heat two teaspoons of oil, add the okra and mix briefly over a medium fire. Sprinkle drops of water and close the top briefly. Eliminate cover and tenderly mix over a medium fire until dull brilliant in color.

3. Heat the leftover oil and pop the mustard. This is optional.

4. Add salt and preparing to the okra.

5. Add yogurt not long prior to serving and blend well.

Tasty Tip: Smear the okras with ½ teaspoon of oil and zap in a microwave on high for two minutes. Remove, stir and cook for half a minute more.

Then season it. Add cleaved cilantro for a new flavor.
SPICY OKRA STIR FRY

vendakkai kari

Prep Time: 10 mins. Serves 3 portions

Spicy Okra Stir Fried

Ingredients:

1 lb okra

¼ tsp turmeric

powder 1 tsp pitlai

powder

2 tsps ground

coconut 8 curry

leaves

¼ tsp salt

For Seasoning:

¼ tsp mustard

seeds 2 tbsps oil

Method:

1. Trim the closures of the okra and cleave it into thick rounds.

2. In a non-stick skillet, heat the oil and pop the mustard. Add the okra and turmeric powder. Mix and sprinkle a little water. Cook for 3-4 minutes. Keep on cooking uncovered.

3. Ensure that the seeds of the okra are cooked and delicate. Presently close and cook briefly. Open mix again and add the pitlai powder, curry leaves and salt and blend gently.

Timely Tip: Optionally cook the okra in the microwave in just a teaspoon of oil. Add all the ingredients together and cook in the microwave for 5-6 minutes. Remove every two minutes, stir and remove finally when done.

OKRA IN LENTIL CURRY

vendakkai sambar

Prep Time: 5 mins. Serves 3 portions

A universal favorite, the okra sambar is an instant pick-me-up, as it rushes fuel to the brain.

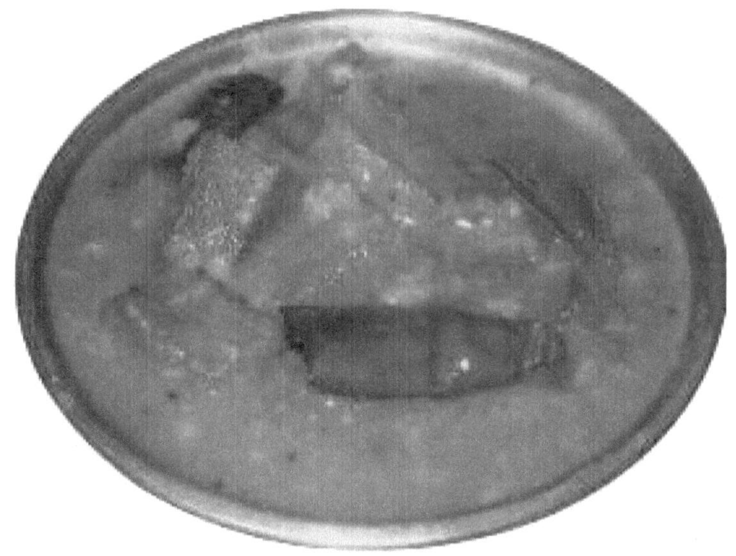

Okra in Lentil Curry

Ingredients:

½ cup pigeon peas/thuvar dal

2 tsps tamarind sauce

½ lb okra

¼ tsp asafetida/hing

powder 1½ tsps sambar

powder

8 curry leaves

1 tbsp coriander leaves

½ tsp salt

For Seasoning:

¼ tsp mustard seeds

2 dried red bean stew, tearing it a little

¼ tsp fenugreek

seeds 1 tsp oil

Method:

1. Trim finishes and split the vegetable.

2. Soak the pigeon peas in steaming hot water for 15 minutes adding a quarter teaspoon of turmeric powder and cook in two cups of water to an exceptionally delicate soft consistency. Then again, pressure-cook on a medium fire for 5-6 whistles. At the point when the strain decreases totally, open the cover and use. (Utilize a huge tension cooker adding some water in the base. Place the dish with the splashed pigeon peas close with a cover. Follow this technique for cooking the pigeon peas for all dishes requiring it).

3. Heat the oil, pop the mustard, and brown the dried red bean stew and fenugreek. Add the okra and mix for a large portion of a moment. Add sambar powder, salt, some water and blend. Cover and stew over a medium fire for five minutes until the vegetable relax, yet remains firm.

4. Add the tamarind mash and asafetida powder. Stew over a medium fire for a few minutes. Add the cooked gram. Whenever it thickens a bit, add wet and squashed curry leaves. Mix and eliminate from fire.

5. Garnish with finely hacked coriander leaves.

OKRA IN TAMARIND SAUCE

vendakkai vathal kuzhambu

Prep Time: 8 mins. Serves 3 portions

Fenugreek is usually added to tamarind-based dishes in Tamil cuisine. It is one of the earliest herbs used in cooking and has great medicinal qualities.

Okra in Tamarind Sauce

Ingredients:

½ lb okra

2 tbsps tamarind sauce

½ tsp asafetida/hing

powder 1½ tbsps sambar

powder

8 curry leaves

1 tbsps sesame oil

½ tsp salt

For The Seasoning:

¼ tsp mustard seeds

¼ tsp fenugreek

seeds 1 tsp sesame

oil

Method:

1. Trim the two sides and cut the okra into a few pieces.

2. Heat a teaspoon of oil, pop the mustard and brown the fenugreek. Add the okra and mix briefly. Add two cups of water, sambar powder, asafetida and salt. Cover and stew for five minutes.

3. Remove the top, add the tamarind sauce and over a medium fire thicken the kuzhambu a little.

4. Add wet squashed curry leaves and the remainder of the sesame oil. Mix and eliminate from flame.

Timely tip: If watery, tie with a tablespoon of rice flour. Mix well to eliminate lumps.

SNAKE GOURD

pudalangai/ chichinda

This long and curved native vegetable resembles snakes hanging from a trellis. The snake gourd plant yields generously, and has been the staple of many Tamil families. To keep the vegetable straight while growing on the plant, a stone is tied to the hanging end. Nowadays, a shorter variety like a cucumber is also available.

According to Ayurveda, it is a Spanish fly and a good de-wormer. It likewise goes about as a diuretic. Snake gourd is an adaptable vegetable and can be made dry or as a curry; it very well may be full, too.

BUYING TIPS

a. The vegetable can become hard and stringy.

b. Watch out for a light green skin.

c. It likewise comes in two shades of green, plain and with stripes.

d. Test for delicacy by severing a tip of the vegetable.

PREPARATION TIPS

a. Cut into quarters the long way, deseed and afterward cut into half moons or quarters.

b. Soak in water to wash away any solid smell that it might emit.

c. Rinse, channel and afterward sauté or bubble it.

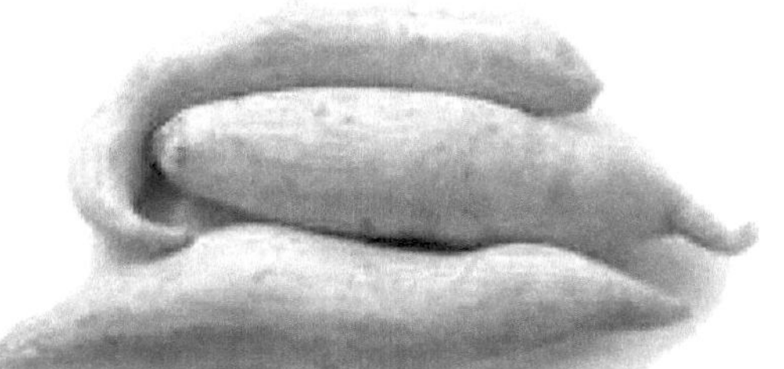

SNAKE GOURD SEASONED IN YOGURT

pudalangai thayir pachadi

Prep Time: 8 mins. Serves 3 portions

This vegetable raita, which goes with any main course meal, is a Tamil Nadu specialty!

Snake Gourd Seasoned in Yogurt

Ingredients:

½ lb snake gourd

2 cups yogurt, beaten

¼ tsp mustard

seeds 1 tsp oil

¼ tsp salt

Make A Coarse Paste With:

2 tbsps ground coconut

1" piece of ginger, peeled

Method:

1. Slit the vegetable, de-seed and slash into little semi-circles. Cleave with the seed if tender.

2. Prepare a coarse glue of the ginger and ground coconut in a blender.

Keep aside.

3. Heat a quarter cup of water with salt in a profound skillet and add the slashed snake gourd. Sauté softly with a spatula until rich green in shading. Close and stew the vegetable over a medium fire for three minutes until exceptionally delicate. Remove the flame.

4. Heat a teaspoon of oil and pop the mustard seeds. Add the popped mustard, the mixed glue and the vegetable to the yogurt. Blend well and fill in as a side dish.

Tasty tip: Use less salt for this vegetable. Discard the seeded middle portion if not tender. Zap the vegetable in a microwave for two to three minutes if you want to save time.

SNAKE GOURD SPICY STIR FRY

pudalangai jeera kari

Prep Time: 10 mins. Serves 3 portions

This bland vegetable can be made interesting with garnishing of coconut and a hint of a red chilli with spices.

Snake Gourd Spicy Stir Fry

Ingredients:

1 lb snake

gourd 6

curry leaves

¼ tsp salt

For The Seasoning:

¼ tsp mustard seeds

½ tsp husked split dark gram/urad dal

1 tsp oil

To Blend Coarsely:

3 tbsps coconut,

ground 1 dried red

chilli

1 tsp cumin seeds

Method:

1. Slit the vegetable, deseed and hack into little pieces.

2. Heat a large portion of a teaspoon of oil and dish the bean
stew until red and firm. Coarsely mix with coconut and cumin
seeds, adding
1-2 teaspoons of water. Keep aside.

3. Heat a large portion of some water in a profound container, add salt
and the cleaved snake gourd. Throw delicately with a spatula until rich
green in shading. Over a medium fire, cover and cook for three
minutes. Open and sauté until delicate however firm. Keep aside.

4. Heat a large portion of a teaspoon of oil in a pan, pop the mustard seeds
and brown the dark gram.

5. Add wet and squashed curry leaves, the cooked vegetable and mixed
glue and sauté over a medium fire for 10 seconds.

*Tasty Tip: Instead of the coarsely blended spices, season it plainly,
adding a halved whole red chilli and a pinch of asafetida powder to the
seasoning.*
*Stir all, eliminate from fire and add a tablespoon or two of ground
coconut. Accept me this has a new and incredible taste.*

SNAKE GOURD CURRY IN A VEGETABLE MELANGE

pudalangai poritha kootu

Prep Time: 12 mins. Serves 4 portions

*Moong dal is totally acceptable to the most orthodox Tamilians. Dishes
with green gram tend to thicken when cooling. Dilute with a little water
and check the salt before serving.*

Snake Gourd Curry in a Vegetable Melange

Ingredients:

¼ cup pigeon peas/thuvar dal

1 lb snake gourd

2 three-inch hacked

drumstick 1 entire eggplant,

cubed

½ tsp salt

For The Paste:

¾ tsp husked split dark gram/urad dal

2 dried red chillis

¼ tsp asafetida/hing

powder 3 tbsps coconut,

grated

For Seasoning:

¼ tsp mustard seeds

½ tsp husked split dark gram/urad dal

6 curry

leaves 1½

tsps oil

Method:

1. Slit the snake gourd, deseed and cleave into little pieces. Utilize the seed if tender.

2. Heat a teaspoon of oil, cook the chillis for five seconds until a dazzling red. Presently brown the husked split dark gram, add asafetida and mix for 5 seconds.

3. Blend with coconut into a coarse paste.

4. Cook the green gram in 1½ cups of water until delicate. Then again, pressure-cook for a whistle. Lower fire and cook for 3-4 minutes.

5. Boil water and salt in two cups of water and cook the slashed vegetables over a medium fire until delicate. Add the mixed glue and cooked gram. Mix delicately and let it bubble and thicken for two minutes. Eliminate from flame.

6. In a little container, heat the excess oil, pop the mustard and daintily brown the dark gram. Wet and smash curry leaves sauté and add to the stewing sauce. Mix for a couple of moments and remove.

SNAKE GOURD PEPPER GRAVY

pudalangai milagu kootu

Prep Time: 10 mins. Serves 3 portions

Snake Gourd Pepper Gravy

Ingredients:

¼ cup husked split green gram/moong dal

1 lb snake gourd/chichinda

¼ tsp asafetida/hing powder

¼ tsp turmeric powder

½ tsp salt

Toast and

Powder: 1 tsp

peppercorns For

Seasoning:

¼ tsp mustard

seeds 6 curry

leaves

1½ tsps oil

Method:

1. Slit the vegetable, deseed and hack into little pieces. On the off chance that delicate, cleave and utilize the seeds. Keep aside.

2. Soak the moong dal in bubbling water for 15 to 20 minutes. Cook until soft.

3. Toast the peppercorns in a large portion of a teaspoon of oil until they pop and the flavors are delivered. Powder and keep aside.

4. Boil two cups of water, adding salt and asafetida. Add the vegetable and throw until a rich green in shading. Allow it to stew over a medium fire until it is delicate. Add the cooked green gram, mixed peppercorn and blend well. Add wet and squashed curry leaves, blend and eliminate from flame.

5. Serve as a primary course with steamed rice.

SNAKE GOURD IN LENTIL CURRY

pudalangai kootu

Prep Time: 12 mins. Serves 4 portions

This curry is full of flavor and very simple to prepare.

Snake Gourd in Lentil Curry

Ingredients:

¼ cup husked split green gram/moong dal

1 lb snake gourd

½ tsp salt

For The Paste:

1 dried red chilli

¼ tsp asafetida/hing

powder 3 tbsps coconut,

grated

1 tbsp cumin seeds

For Seasoning:

¼ tsp mustard seeds

½ tsp husked split dark gram/urad dal

6 curry

leaves 1½

tsps oil

Method:

1. Slit the vegetable, deseed and hack into little pieces.

2. Heat a teaspoon of oil, cook the bean stew for five seconds until a dazzling red. Presently add asafetida to mix for three seconds. Mix these with coconut and cumin into a paste.

3. Cook the green gram in 1½ cups of water until delicate. Alternatively, pressure-cook for a whistle. Lower fire and cook for 3-4 minutes. Whenever the strain decreases totally, open and use.

4. Boil 2 cups of water with salt and cook the slashed vegetable over a medium fire until delicate and tender.

5. Add the mixed glue and cooked gram, mix delicately and permit it to bubble for two minutes. Thicken and eliminate from flame.

6. In a little dish, heat the excess oil, pop the mustard and daintily brown the dark gram.

7. Wet and pulverize curry leaves, sauté and add to the stewing sauce. Mix for a couple of moments and remove.

AMARANTH

keerai/ palak

Keerai is the Tamil word for leafy vegetables like spinach. Different varieties are available in India, particularly in Tamil Nadu. The amaranth is a leafy vegetable that is an excellent source of vitamins A, B6 and C and riboflavin and iron. It also contains the minerals calcium, iron, magnesium, phosphorus, potassium, zinc, copper, and manganese. Iron levels in amaranth leaves are three times more than in spinach. The edible tender leaves and stems can be cooked like spinach. It contains in saturated fat and is very low in cholesterol.

BUYING TIPS

a. Amaranth leaves are available as a green and red variety.

b. The green leaves can be pointed or rounded.

c. The leaves should be a radiant green and crisp.

d. If it looks withered and dry, it is old stock.

PREPARATION TIPS

a. Most regularly, the greens accompany the roots.

b. Cut or pluck out the lower part of the plant.

c. Wash completely in a colander, channel the water and afterward flush again a few times under running water to guarantee that all the mud is washed out.

d. Chop the greens fine alongside the stem.

e. Stems and leaves that might be more developed can be utilized in curries.

AMARANTH LENTIL CURRY

keerai sambhar

Prep Time: 8 mins. Serves 3 portions

The goodness of greens made palatable to fussy eaters.

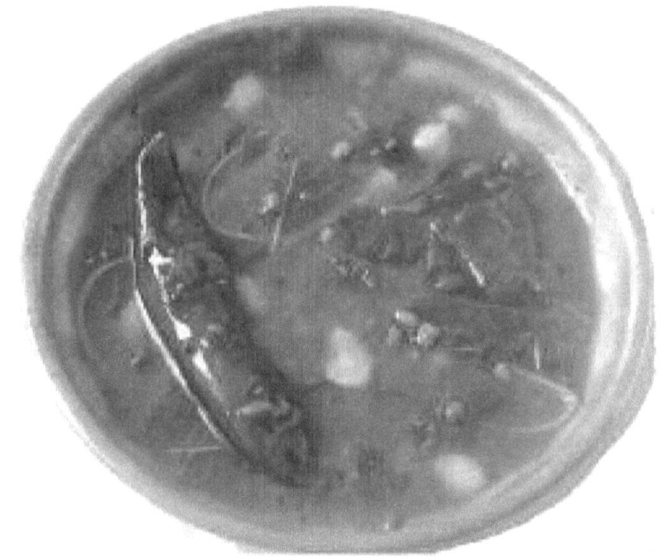

Amaranth Lentil Curry

Ingredients:

1 pack spinach, washed and chopped

¼ cup pigeon peas/thuvar dal

1½ tsps tamarind sauce

1½ tsps sambar powder

½ tsp salt

For Seasoning:

¼ tsp mustard seeds

½ tsp asafetida/hing powder

¼ tsp fenugreek

seeds 1 tsp oil

Method:

1. Cook the pigeon peas in 2½ cups of water till they is soft. On the other hand, pressure cook for a whistle and lower fire to stew for four minutes. Whenever the strain totally decreases, open and use.

2. Heat the oil, pop the mustard and brown the fenugreek seeds. Add the asafetida powder. Keep aside.

3. Add the spinach and salt alongside 1½ cups of water. Stew for 3 - 4 minutes until the spinach is delicate. Add the sambar powder and the cooked pigeon peas. Add the carefully prepared mustard and cook for a few minutes over a medium fire or until it thickens to sauce consistency.

Tasty Tip: Use okra, ash gourd, drumstick, pumpkin, etc., to prepare this authentic sambar.

AMARANTH IN CRUMBLED LENTIL

keerai usili

Amaranth in Crumbled Lentil

Prep Time: 8 mins. Serves 3 portions

Method:

1. Wash, slash and sautéed food the amaranth with somewhat salt, sprinkling a couple of drops of water. Eliminate from fire in a few minutes. Keep aside.

2. Make a steamed lentil disintegrate and add to the pan-seared amaranth. Follow the lentil disintegrate method as given for severe gourd, wide beans or bunch beans.

SPICY AMARANTH IN YOGURT

mor keerai

Prep Time: 12 mins. Serves 4 portions

This is an unusual combination of yogurt and spinach made into a curry.

Spicy Amaranth in Yogurt

Ingredients:

1 pack amaranth, slashed fine

2 cups yogurt, beaten in ¾ cup of water

¼ tsp asafetida/hing powder

½ tsp salt

For The Paste:

1 tbsp rice, absorbed heated

water 3 tbsps coconut, grated

2 green chillis

For Seasoning:

¼ tsp mustard

seeds 1 tsp oil

Method:

1. Permit rice to splash for 15 - 20 minutes before you mix with the coconut and green chillis into a fine glue utilizing 1 - 2 tablespoons of water.

2. In a profound container, heat up some water adding salt. Add the washed and hacked greens with the asafetida powder and throw with a scoop until wealthy in shading. Cover and stew over a medium fire for 4 - 5 minutes. Strain the water and squash the greens into a coarse mass.

3. In a profound container, heat the oil and pop the mustard. Add the greens squash, mixed glue, yogurt and popped mustard. Stew over a medium fire, mixing for several minutes.

4. Serve hot with steamed rice.

Tasty Tip: Add half a teaspoon of browned fenugreek seeds to the seasoning for a different flavor.

AMARANTH IN TAMARIND SAUCE

puli keerai

Prep Time: 10 mins. Serves 4 portions

This is a popular and tangy dish from Tanjore that goes with yogurt gravies.

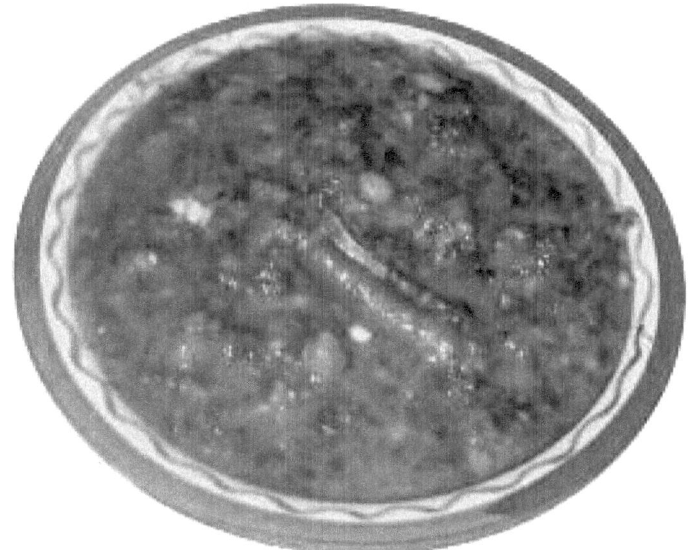

Amaranth in Tamarind Sauce

Ingredients:

2 packs amaranth, cut fine

½ cup pigeon peas/thuvar dal

2 tbsps tamarind sauce

3 green chillis, slit

½ tsp asafetida/hing powder

½ tsp salt

For Seasoning:

¼ tsp mustard seeds

½ tsp bengal gram/chana dal

½ tsp oil

Method:

1. Cook the pigeon peas in 2½ cups of water until they turn soft. Then again, pressure cook for a whistle and lower fire to cook further for 10 minutes. Switch off and when the strain diminishes, totally open and use.

2. In a profound skillet, heat up some water, adding salt. Add the washed and slashed greens with the asafetida powder and green chillis, and throw with a spoon until wealthy in shading. Cover and stew over a medium fire for 4 - 5 minutes until delicate. Strain the water and utilizing a hand crush, squash it coarsely and set aside.

3. Heat the oil, pop the mustard, add and gently brown the bengal gram. Add the greens, tamarind sauce and the cooked lentil. Cook for three minutes over a medium fire or until the sauce thickens marginally. In the event that excessively thick, add a portion of the stressed water and mix for two or three minutes.

Important Point: Some varieties of chillis are too spicy so use less. Alternatively, de-seed before using.

FENUGREEK LEAVES

vendhaya keerai/ methi bajhi

This verdant vegetable is notable for its therapeutic properties. It lessens stomach and stomach related problems, weakness, respiratory contaminations, diabetes and cancer.

The youthful leaves and fledglings of fenugreek are eaten as greens. The new or dried leaves are utilized to enhance dishes. The dried leaves (called kasuri methi) have a somewhat harsh taste however by and by, have a solid flavor.
When utilizing dried fenugreek, pulverize it hard in the center of your hand and afterward add.

BUYING TIPS

a. There are two kinds of fenugreek leaves-enormous plants with huge leaves and the little bundles with white roots and little green leaves. The huge ones are accessible normally in the north and the little ones are utilized in South Indian cooking.

b. Check for newness by the freshness of the leaves.

c. Do not buy whenever withered or yellowing.

PREPARATION TIPS

a. The more modest assortment will in general ruin rapidly.

b. Keep the leaves new by cleaving of the roots and isolating the leaves on paper or in a vessel. Cover and refrigerate.

c. Use them inside 24 hours.

d. Just prior to cooking, absorb the leaves water and afterward wash them in a colander in running water until clean.

FENUGREEK LEAF-DRUMSTICK CURRY

vendhiya keerai-murungakkai sambar

Prep Time: 10 mins. Serves 4 portions

An imaginative combination of two vegetables, both rich in iron.

Fenugreek Leaves Drumstick Curry

Ingredients:

½ cup pigeon peas/thuvar dal

2 cleaved drumsticks pieces, 3"

long 2 cups fenugreek leaves

2 tsps tamarind sauce

¼ tsp asafetida/hing

powder 1½ tsps sambar

powder

½ tsp salt

For Seasoning:

¼ tsp mustard

seeds 1 tsp oil

Method:

1. Dissolve in two cups of high temp water and splash the pigeon peas for 15 - 20 minutes prior to cooking them in medium hotness until mushy.

2. Alternatively, pressure-cook for a whistle, bring down the fire and cook for 10 minutes. Switch off the fire. Whenever the tension lessens totally, open and use.

3. In a profound dish, add some water, the drumsticks, sambar powder, asafetida powder and salt and cook over a medium fire for 8 - 10 minutes.

4. If the drumstick is overcooked, it will deteriorate; the external skin that is unappetizing can be aggravating and creates problems while gulping. Add the tamarind sauce and mix tenderly for several minutes.

5. Add washed and hacked fenugreek leaves, cooked lentil and bubble over a medium fire for two minutes or until the sauce thickens.

6. Heat the oil and pop the mustard. Add to the gravy.

Timely Tip: You can even add ash gourd or bottle gourd to this sambar. Pressure-cook the lentil and store in small portions in the freezer. Use whenever needed for a dish.

GREEN BERRY/ TURKEY BERRY

manathakkali/ sundakkai

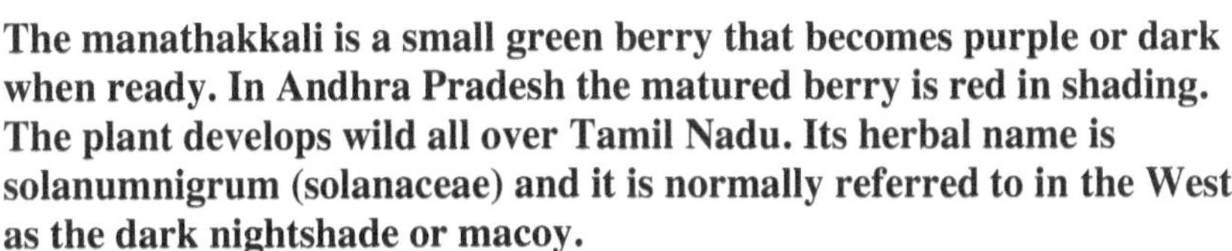

The manathakkali is a small green berry that becomes purple or dark when ready. In Andhra Pradesh the matured berry is red in shading. The plant develops wild all over Tamil Nadu. Its herbal name is solanumnigrum (solanaceae) and it is normally referred to in the West as the dark nightshade or macoy.

The little berry is culled, singed and made in to vatthal or dried food. It is utilized as a therapeutic spice, cooked in explained spread/ghee and eaten with rice or included curries and flavors. Its particular flavor and smell gives the well known dish vathal kuzhambu an interesting character. It can likewise be utilized to blend in with steamed rice. The plant has egg-molded, elliptic leaves that are cooked and filled in as a side dish. The leaves are somewhat harsh, which turns out to be less articulated in the wake of cooking. These leaves, known as Manathakkali keerai are utilized to address sustenance problems for "stomatitis" or aggravation of the stomach, gastrointestinal and mouth ulcers. Manathakkali, both new and dried, is utilized as a diuretic and further develops hunger. Manathakkali leaves are valuable in fevers; a soup produced using it goes about as a cooling drink; it makes you sweat. The leaf of the manathakkali contains 5.9% of protein, 1.0% of fat, 2.1% of minerals and 8.9% of carbs per four ounces. It contains minerals and nutrients like calcium, phosphorus, iron, riboflavin, niacin, and L-ascorbic acid. Its calorific worth is 68. As the manathakkali plant develops out of control, its leaves can without much of a stretch be culled and utilized for scrumptious dishes. The leaves mix well with different greens and dals.

The turkey berry or sundakai (solanum torvum) has a place with the solanaceae family. This berry is involved new or dried the same way just like the dark nightshade. Generally, these two varieties of berries are lightly pounded, then added and mixed with yogurt and salt. They are then left

out in the sun to dry. While the drying system is finished, they are put away in bottles. As an ayurvedic spice, the turkey berry has narcotic, diuretic and stomach related properties. It used to treat hacks, and is a tonic for the liver. The turkey berry in its new structure is utilized to make a sambar or a sautéed food kari while the dried berry is scrumptious when pan-seared and added to steamed rice, and in making a vathal kuzhambu.

FRESH TURKEY BERRY CURRY

sundakkai sambar

Prep Time: 10 mins. Serves 3 portions

The versatile sambar can be made with any vegetable. Every vegetable adds a unique flavor to sambars. The mild flavoring of this cuisine adds to the glorious taste of the dish.

Fresh Turkey Berry Curry

Ingredients:

½ cup pigeon peas/thuvar dal

1½ tsps tamarind

sauce 4 oz new turkey

berries

¼ tsp asafetida/hing

powder 1½ tsps sambar

powder

10 curry leaves

½ bundle coriander leaves, optional

½ tsp salt

For The Seasoning:

¼ tsp mustard seeds

¼ tsp fenugreek

seeds 1 tsp oil

Method:

1. Smash the new berries with a weighty mortar so it opens up.

2. Soak the pigeon peas in steaming hot water for 10 minutes and cook in 2½ cups of water to a squash. On the other hand, pressure-cook for a whistle, lower fire and cook for 10 minutes. Whenever the tension lessens, totally open and use.

3. Heat the oil, pop the mustard then, at that point, add the fenugreek seeds to brown. Add asafetida powder and eliminate. Add the berries and sauté for a minute.

4. Now add sambar powder and some water. Cover and stew over a medium fire for 10 minutes until the berry is cooked.

5. Add the tamarind purée and salt. Cook for a few minutes. Add the cooked lentil. Whenever it thickens marginally, eliminate from fire.

6. Finally, add wet squashed curry leaves, mix for 30 seconds and trimming with finely cleaved coriander leaves.

TURKEY BERRY TANGY SAUCE

sundakkai vathal kuzhambu

Prep Time: 10 mins. Serves 3 portions

This wonder berry can be prepared using fresh berries or dried and salted ones. This dish is prepared using the dried salted ones. Dried turkey berries and black nightshade are available in most Indian groceries.

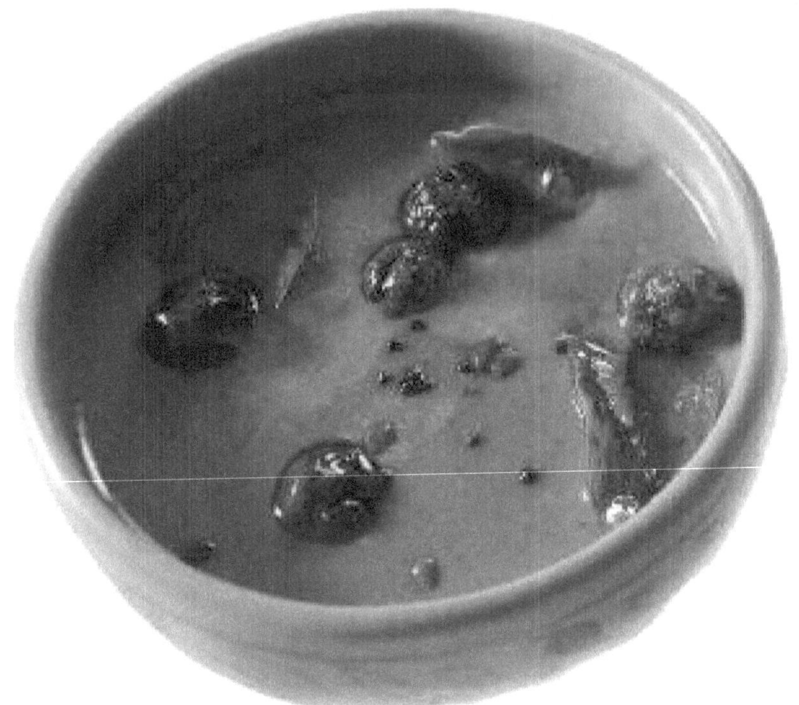

Turkey Berry Tangy Sauce

Ingredients:

2 tbsps dried turkey

berry 1 tbsps tamarind

sauce 1½ tsps sambar

powder

½ tsp earthy colored sugar, optional

¼ teaspoon asafetida/hing powder

¼ tsp turmeric powder

¼ tsp salt

A touch of brown sugar

For seasoning:

¼ tsp mustard seeds

1 dried red bean

stew, split 1

teaspoon oil

1 tablespoon explained margarine/ghee

Method:

1. Heat a teaspoon of oil, pop the mustard and mix in the divided stew. Add the berry and sauté delicately briefly. Whenever it is sautéed a little, mix in the tamarind purée, some water, the asafetida powder, sambar powder, and salt.

2. Cover and stew for 8 - 10 minutes. Thicken into a light sauce, blending in earthy colored sugar and wet squashed curry leaves.

3. Stir for five seconds. Add the leftover sesame oil and eliminate from fire.

4. Serve as primary course with steamed rice and a green vegetable. This sauce can be put away in a cooler and utilized north of a couple days.

Note: This recipe is good for all vathal kuzhambus.

Prepare a primary course dish with dried green berry utilizing a similar strategy. Dark nightshade or macoy berry can be ready similarly as the turkey berry, extremely local and very tasty.

TURKEY BERRY RICE

sundakkai sadham

Prep Time: 8 mins. Serves 2 portions

Method:

1. Pound a bit and pan fried food the dried, salted turkey berry in two tablespoons of ghee briefly. Blend in with steamed rice. The sharpness of these berries gives an additional flavor to the rice. Beating is fundamental as the salt and the flavor is all around blended in with the tasteless rice.

2. Squeeze in wet curry leaves. Present with banana or potato wafers.

Turkey Berry Rice

Note: Dried berries are available in packets in the Indian or Asian food. The vathal kuzhambu can be made with a large group of vegetables each adding its own singular taste to the kuzhambu/sauce.

FOUR VARIETY SPINACH KARI

kalavan keerai

Prep Time: 10 mins. Serves 3 portions

A mélange of different greens seasoned and garnished with freshly grated coconut.

Four Variety Spinach Kari

Ingredients:

4 cups each manathakkali, molai keerai, ara keerai and siru keerai (all spinach varieties)

½ tsp sambar powder

¼ tsp asafetida/hing powder

¼ tsp turmeric powder

¼ tsp salt

A touch of brown sugar

For Seasoning:

¼ tsp mustard seeds

½ tsp husked split dark gram/urad dal

1 tbsp coconut,

ground 1 tsp oil

Method:

1. Pluck the spinach leaves, disposing of the green berry, dark night conceal or manathakkali. Wash well in a colander, cleave generally, add and blend turmeric, sambar powder, asafetida and salt. Keep aside.

2. Heat the oil, pop the mustard and gently brown the dark gram. Add all to the greens.

3. Over a medium fire, mix in an open container and permit it to stew briefly. At the point when the water dissipates, add the sugar and the ground coconut. Blend gently, permitting the flavors to mix well. Eliminate from flame.

FRESH PICKLED CHILI SALAD

mor milagai

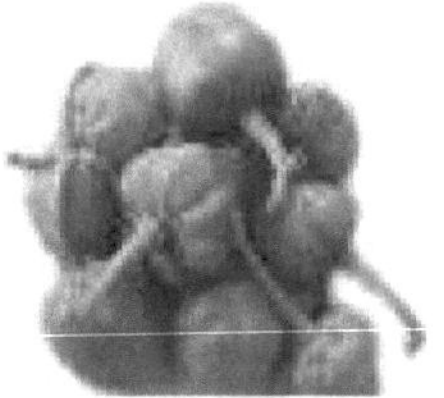

Tangy and utterly tasty, these pickled chilies are most famous in the southern part of India. You cannot resist a 'mor milagai' with yogurt and rice.

Method:

1. For a quarter half pound of Indian green chilies utilize six tablespoons of beaten yogurt. Punch holes in all sides of the green bean stew. This guarantees that the flavors and the yogurt marinates well and in the inner parts as well. Blend in 1½ teaspoons of squashed stone salt or a teaspoonful of table salt. Mix well with the green stew and dry in the sun.

2. Mix it well again and dry it again during the day. You might even microwave it for two minutes. Eliminate, blend again and return to the microwave for two additional minutes until the covering of yogurt evaporates. Refrigerate.

3. Take a couple of chilies, profound fry in oil until they turn a dull brown and firm. Add them to yogurt and rice.

4. They have an awesome, tart hot pungent taste. A few homes toast, powder and add some fenugreek seeds to give them an additional local taste. However, this is optional.

Tasty Tip: Follow the same method to prepare with fresh macoy or fresh turkey berries.

MIXED VEGETABLES

What do you do when you have an assortment of vegetables left over in pieces and pieces? Combine them as one and make a vegetable mélange.

The avial is generally made with explicit vegetables. You can substitute any vegetable with what you have in the cooler other than okra! The avial is depicted in my book, 'Samayal'.

The blended vegetable kootu is generally cooked for merry events like Thiruvadirai and Pongal. Current life is tied in with adjusting and compromising-so feel free to assemble the pieces and bits of vegetables extra in your fridge and serve them generally up with spirit as a stew that can be eaten with rice, roti or bread!

A FESTIVAL MELANGE GRAVY

thiruvadharai kootu

Prep Time: 12-14 mins. Serves 3 portions

A winter dish cooked for Lord Siva's festival with vegetables that are available in season.

A Festival Melange Gravy

Ingredients:

1½ tbsps tamarind sauce

10 wide beans

3 little Indian eggplants

½ piece debris gourd or jug gourd

¼ piece red pumpkin

1 cup field beans, shelled

1 enormous unripe green

banana 1 medium-sized

sweet potato

3 green chillis, cut lengthwise

¼ tsp turmeric powder

¼ tsp asafetida

powder 1 tsp

sambar powder

¾ tsp salt

For Seasoning:

¼ tsp mustard seeds

¼ tsp husked split dark gram

½ cup ground

coconut 8 curry

leaves

2 tbsps oil

Method:

1. Peel off the skins of the debris gourd, pumpkin, yam, and green banana. Dice every one of the vegetables into medium-sized cubes.

2. Top and tail wide beans and cleave into 2-3 pieces.

3. Boil 1½ cups of water, adding salt in a profound dish. Over a medium fire, add vegetables, Green chillis, turmeric, asafetida and sambar powder. Close top and cook for 6-7 minutes or until the vegetables are delicate yet firm. Add the tamarind concentrate, mix and bubble for two additional minutes. Keep aside.

4. Heat the oil, pop the mustard seeds and brown the dark gram. Brown the coconut by simmering it for three minutes. At long last, add the vegetables and mix for two minutes until the sauce thickens.

5. Wet smash the curry leaves and mix into the thickened sauce. Eliminate and fill in as a side dish.

Tasty Tip: The shelled field beans can be replaced with fresh soya beans, soaked and cooked kabuli/ chick peas or brown gram. Add a spoonful of the pitlai powder finally and augment the taste quotient! The very popular dish in a Tamil home 'avial' is described in my book

OLD HABITS DIE HARD: REVISITING TRADITION

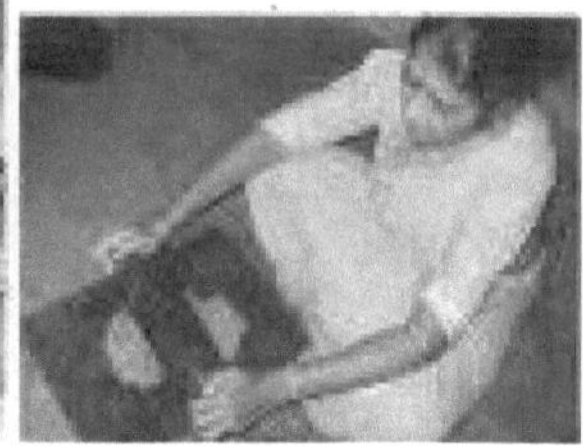

Cutting vegetables or preparing food was finished hunching down on the floor. An extremely sound propensity that is as yet done in unassuming communities and in a few metropolitan homes. Yoga prescribes crouching on the floor to hack vegetables and cooking as it helps in adjusting the blood flow in our body. Player crushing is a cool movement. It is great actual exercise, and you can feel the surface of the player while crushing. An electric blender can never accomplish this flawlessness. Our concerns started with current contraptions, which we presently accept have become key. This idea is false as it is just for the expert young lady in a rush to get to her working environment. Shouldn't something be said about the other home-creators who don't do this any longer? This is our custom, our lifestyle our way of life, our way of life. We should not lose it any longer than we as of now have. Dear companions, this is the kind of thing I feel emphatically about.

Implements utilized in a customary home. An iron vegetable shaper and a stone processor used to powder grains that were washed and dried and spread on a cheddar fabric to eliminate the wetness before powdering.

GREEN BANANA

vazhakkai/ kacha kela

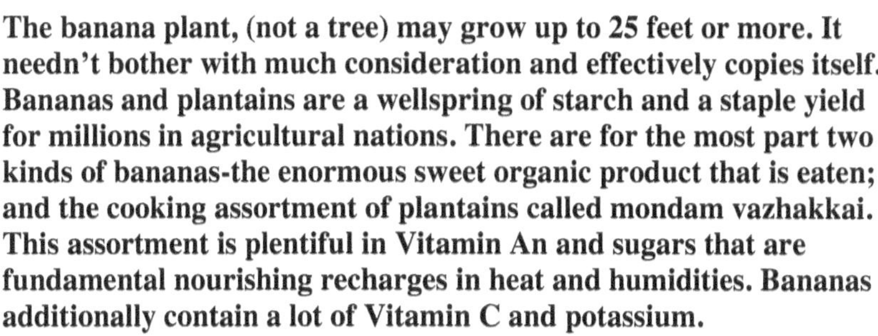

The banana plant, (not a tree) may grow up to 25 feet or more. It needn't bother with much consideration and effectively copies itself. Bananas and plantains are a wellspring of starch and a staple yield for millions in agricultural nations. There are for the most part two kinds of bananas-the enormous sweet organic product that is eaten; and the cooking assortment of plantains called mondam vazhakkai. This assortment is plentiful in Vitamin An and sugars that are fundamental nourishing recharges in heat and humidities. Bananas additionally contain a lot of Vitamin C and potassium.

In Asia, all aspects of the banana plant is used for different purposes. The leaves are utilized as eating surfaces, for cooking and wrapping. The dampness in the passes on assists with keeping food new for a more drawn out time frame. The green leaves are skillfully collapsed into cups or donnais and used to serve curries and fluids. Food served or cooked in banana leaves ingests the flavor and smell from the leaves, adding to the flavor of the meal.

BUYING TIPS

a. The crude banana should be full and green.

b. Any indications of yellowing implies that it has begun to mature and the inner parts will be gooey.

PREPARATION TIPS

a. Chop off the stem and tail and strip the crude banana till you arrive at the white piece of the vegetable.

b. Immediately submerge in chilly water to forestall discoloring.

c. Cut every banana into the expected shape and return it to the water.

d. After the flavoring is prepared, remove the pieces from the water and straightforwardly move to the wok.

e. Green banana leaves are utilized to cover a container while cooking and as a surface to steam different dishes. The foods grown from the ground are an essential piece of Tamil cooking. It is said that the monks who lived in the woods lived on a consistent eating routine of bananas until they became saints.

STIR FRIED BANANA

vazhakai vadhakal

Prep Time: 10 mins. Serves 3 portions

Stir Fried Banana

Ingredients:

2 medium-sized crude bananas

½ tsp sambar powder

¼ tsp asafetida/hing powder

½ tsp salt

For Seasoning:

¼ tsp mustard

seeds 3 tbsps oil

Method:

1. Peel the crude banana and cleave it into quarter inch shapes. Keep them in a bowl of water to stay away from discoloration.

2. Heat oil in a non-stick container and pop the mustard. Channel the water, add the hacked vegetable and the curry leaves and mix delicately.

Cover and stew over medium hotness for two or three minutes.

3. Open the top and mix until the vegetable is delicate and done. Add the sambar powder, asafetida powder and salt. Mix tenderly so it doesn't become uneven. Add an additional a teaspoon of oil on the off chance that it is too dry.

Timely Tip: Optionally you could use roasted crushed red pepper/ chilli flakes instead of sambar powder. Grated coconut is also added as a garnish by some Tamil homes.

SPICY BANANA MASH

vazhakai kozhasa kari

Prep Time: 10 mins. Serves 3 portions

A mushy side dish that tastes good and unusual.

Spicy Banana Mash

Ingredients:

2 medium-sized crude

bananas 1 tbsp tamarind

sauce

¼ tsp asafetida/hing powder

¼ tsp turmeric powder

6 curry leaves

½ tsp salt

For Seasoning:

¼ tsp mustard seeds

¼ tsp husked split dark gram/urad dal

4 dried red chillis,

divicied 2 tbsps oil

Method:

1. Peel the banana and hack into quarters of half-inch thickness. Keep the slashed vegetable in a bowl of water to stay away from discoloration.

2. Boil some water in a profound dish. Add the vegetable in the wake of depleting the water it has been kept in, the turmeric powder and salt. Cover and stew over heat for five minutes until it is delicate however firm. Add the tamarind mash and bubble for a few minutes.

3. In a pot, heat the oil, pop the mustard and brown the dark gram. Add the red chillis and fry until dazzling red and firm. Add to the stewing vegetable and blend tenderly. Wet and pulverize curry leaves and add with asafetida powder. Mix for a minute.

4. Remove from fire and fill in as a side dish with steamed rice.

TANGY BANANA CRUMBLE

vazhakai podimas

Prep Time: 5 mins. Serves 3 portions

Deliciously Tamil in taste, it is an easy and healthy dish.

Tangy Banana Crumble

Ingredients:

2 medium-sized crude bananas

2-3 medium-sized green

chillis 2"piece of ginger,

grated

2 tbps lime/lemon juice

½ tsp salt

For Seasoning:

¼ tsp mustard seeds

½ tsp husked split dark gram/urad dal

3 tbps coconut,

ground 6 curry

leaves

1 tsp oil

Method:

1. Chop vegetable with skin into 2 - 3 pieces.

2. Chop the green chillis. Keep aside.

3. Cover and cook the banana in two cups of water for 5-6 minutes or until the skin turns dull and the vegetable turns out to be delicate. Test for delicate quality by puncturing the open side of the vegetable with a fork.

4. Peel and dispose of skin. Disintegrate with hand or mesh in a carrot grater. Keep aside.

5. In a profound wok, heat oil to pop the mustard and brown the gram. Add the green chillis, ginger, and salt. Mix tenderly for five seconds.

6. Now add the curry leaves and the disintegrated vegetable. Sprinkle lime squeeze and blend all that gently.

7. Remove from fire, throw in ground coconut and blend well.

8. Serve this delightful vegetable as a side with a principle course meal.

BANANA TAMARIND CURRY

vazhakai puli kootu

Puli kootus made with raw banana, banana stem and spinach were a specialty in my in-law's home. My mom-in-law was adept in teaching the perfect techniques for this dish or any other dish of this cuisine. We were all spoilt with good food.

Banana Tamarind Curry

Ingredients:

2 medium-sized crude

bananas 1 tbsp tamarind

sauce

¾ tsp sambar powder

½ tsp turmeric powder

¼ tsp asafetida/hing powder

½ cup ground

coconut 12 curry

leaves

½ tsp salt

For Seasoning:

¼ tsp mustard seeds

¼ tsp husked split dark gram/urad dal

2 tsps oil

Method:

1. Cook the pigeon peas as trained in the start of this chapter.

2. After stripping the green skin off totally, cleave the bananas into blocks; absorb them water to stay away from discoloration.

3. Drain the water and cook the vegetable in some water, adding sambar powder, a quarter teaspoon of turmeric powder, asafetida powder and salt. Cover and stew for six minutes or until delicate and done.

4. Add the tamarind sauce and cooked lentil and keep on stewing over a medium fire for two minutes.

5. In another dish, heat the oil, pop the mustard and brown the dark gram. Add ground coconut and sauté until light brown and dried up. Add this to the stewing vegetable.

6. Squeeze wet curry leaves, add and stew for 30 seconds.

7. Serve hot with steamed rice and a sautéed green vegetable of your choice.

BANANA FLOWER

vazhaipoo

BUYING TIPS

a. The flower is a purple, pear shaped vegetable that tapers to a pointed end.

b. It has many slight layers that can be stripped off like the petals of a rose.

PREPARATION TIPS

a. Peel off the various layers of the banana flower.

b. Discard the purple petal layers.

c. Between each layer, you will find a group of finger length flowers.

d. Pluck them from the white focal stem.

e. Remove the spine from the focal point of each blossom (called kallan (the cheat) in Tamil cautiously and dispose of it.

f. Hold the rose bundle in the left hand and hack it finely.

g. Soak in weakened buttermilk to stay away from discoloration.

h. You might utilize the white stem of the entire purple bloom on the off chance that it is tender.

i. Wash the vegetable until the water is clear, channel and add to the flavoring and cook.

j. Some sap might adhere to your hands.

k. Smear your hands with a little cooking oil and wash it off with soap.

BANANA FLOWER IN STEAMED LENTIL

vazhapoo usili

Prep Time: 12-14 mins. Serves 4 portions

The 'Paruppu Usili' increases the quantity of a prepared dish. A classic value addition. Follow instructions to chop banana flowers given in the previous page.

Banana Flower in Steamed Lentil

Ingredients:

½ banana blossoms, hacked fine

¼ tsp brown sugar

½ tsp salt

For the seasoning

¼ tsp mustard

seeds 8 curry

leaves

1 tsp sesame oil/oil

For The Usili:

1 cup pigeon peas/thuvar dal

5 - 6 dried red chillis

½ tsp asafetida/hing powder

¼ tsp turmeric powder

½ tsp salt

Soak the pigeon peas in steaming hot water (enough to cover the lentil) for around 20 minutes.

Blend coarsely alongside different elements for the usili.

Steam for around 10 minutes in a rice cooker or smooth the usili and zap in the microwave for 2 - 3 minutes.

Insert a wooden pick/fork; when it tells the truth, the usili is

finished. Cool the steamed pigeon peas and disintegrate without

lumps.

Method:

1. Heat the oil and pop the mustard. Add the usili combination and mix well for 3 - 4 minutes. Set aside.

2. Heat two cups of water, adding salt. Cook the slashed banana blossom over a medium fire for 5 - 6 minutes with the cover shut for the primary two or three minutes.

3. Open and mix and cook until delicate. Channel off overabundance water.

4. Add the cooked banana blossom and the earthy colored sugar (discretionary). Delicately mix for two minutes over medium hotness. Add more salt whenever required. Mix for 2 - 3 minutes until delicate and crumbly.

5. Add wet and squashed curry leaves, sauté and remove.

Tasty Tip: How do you react when you prepare the queen of all usilis? Ecstatic of course. Not many homes prepare this usili these days as it is a laborious task to open it up chop steam and cook it. The vazhaipoo usili has a unique flavor. With a little love and care it turns out to be a wonderful Tambram food full of nutrition, and health benefits. Please try out this comfort food in the sacred domain of your kitchen. I do not want to add turmeric to the banana flower as I would like to see it in its natural color.

BANANA STEM

vazhaithandu

The banana stem has therapeutic employments. It should have extraordinary characteristics to crush stones in the kidney and nerve bladder.

BUYING TIPS

a. The banana stem resembles a velvety, long, fat and adjusted baton.

b. The stem is sold in the market as foot-long pieces.

c. The skin might be stained, yet check for its delicacy by squeezing a piece of the top focus of the vegetable.

d. If it falls off effectively without extremely long strings of fiber connected, then, at that point, it is tender.

PREPARATION TIPS

a. There is a unique workmanship to setting up the stem for cooking.

b. Peel off the external skin of the banana stem layer by layer until you arrive at the core of the vegetable.

c. Chop into slight round cuts and eliminate the internal fiber between each cut by moving the strings around your pointer. Dispose of the fiber.

d. Chop the cuts into juliennes and afterward into minuscule grain-like pieces.

e. Soak the vegetable in flimsy, harsh buttermilk to keep away from staining before you start to cook.

f. Strain and dispose of the buttermilk water before cooking.

BANANA STEM IN SEASONED YOGURT

vazhathandu thayir pachadi

Prep Time: 12-14 mins. Serves 4 portions

The banana stem can also be added to a raita. The South Indian version of a raita is cooked vegetables added to beaten yogurt with a pinch of salt.

Banana Stem in Seasoned Yogurt

Ingredients:

7-8" long banana stem

2 cups   yogurt, beaten

¼ tsp mustard

Seeds 1 tsp oil

¼ tsp salt

For The Paste:

3 tbsps coconut, ground/frozen

1 green chilli

Method:

1. Prepare a coarse glue of the green stew and ground coconut. Keep aside.

2. Peel the external skin of the banana stem to about a large portion of an inch, cleave into flimsy round cuts and afterward make meager cuts one inch round. Eliminate the inward fiber by moving it in your index finger and dispose of it.

3. Soak in meager buttermilk to stay away from discoloration.

4. Heat a quarter cup of water with salt in a profound dish; wash, channel and add the banana stem. Close and stew the vegetable over a medium fire for 3-4 minutes until delicate and crunchy. Remove the fire and channel the water.

5. Heat a teaspoon of oil, pop the mustard seeds and brown the dark gram. Add it with the mixed glue, yogurt and the vegetable.

6. Serve as a side dish.

BANANA STEM KARI WITH SPICES

vazhathandu kari

Prep Time: 12 mins. Serves 4 portions

When a banana tree was cut in the backyard after it had given fruit, the stem was used in a variety of dishes.

Banana Stem Kari with Spices

Ingredients:

2 tbsps husked split green gram/moong dal

7-8" long banana stem

¼ tsp turmeric powder, optional

¼ tsp asafetida/hing

powder 2 tbsps coconut,

grated

¼ tsp salt

For Seasoning:

¼ tsp mustard seeds

¼ tsp husked split dark gram/urad dal

2 green chillis,

cut 5 curry

leaves

1 tsp oil

Method:

1. Parboil the green gram in two cups of water for 7-10 minutes until half done. Follow the past formula for slashing and splashing this vegetable.

2. Heat the oil, pop the mustard, delicately brown the dark gram and sauté the chillis. Add a large portion of some water, adding salt, turmeric powder and asafetida powder.

3. Add the banana stem and cook for seven minutes or until delicate to taste. Add wet and squashed curry leaves, parboiled moong dal and mix for 30 seconds.

5. Decorate with coconut. Blend well and eliminate from flame.

Tasty Tip: If banana stem is not available, prepare this dish with either raw bananas or snake gourd.

BANANA STEM CURRY

vazhathandu kootu

Prep Time: 12 mins. Serves 4 portions

A very traditional and crunchy tasting curry. Easy to prepare if the pigeon peas are cooked and kept in the freezer.

Banana Stem Curry

Ingredients:

2 tbsps pigeon peas/thuvar dal

7-8" long banana stem

¼ tsp asafetida/hing

powder 7 curry leaves

¼ tsp salt

Prepare A Coarse Paste With:

2 tbsps coconut,

ground 1 green

chilli

1 tsp cumin seeds

For Seasoning:

¼ tsp mustard seeds

¼ tsp husked split dark gram/urad dal

1 tsp oil

Method:

1. Dissolve the pigeon peas in adequate hot water for 15 - 20 minutes.

2. Boil in two cups of water until soft or pressure-cook with little water for one whistle.

3. Lower fire and permit to stew for 10 minutes. At the point when strain lessens totally, open cover and use.

4. Heat the oil, pop the mustard and daintily brown the dark gram. Add a large portion of some water, adding salt, turmeric powder, and asafetida powder.

5. Add the stem and cook for seven minutes or until delicate to taste.

6. Add the coarse glue, popped mustard, seared dark gram and the cooked lentil and let it stew for a few minutes until it transforms into a light sauce.

7. Add wet and squashed curry leaves mix and eliminate. Fill in as a side dish.

BANANA STEM IN TAMARIND SAUCE

vazhathandu puli kootu

Prep Time: 12 mins. Serves 3 portions

My grandmother's simple and tangy recipe, crunchy in every bite!

Banana Stem in Tamarind Sauce

Ingredients:

7-8" long banana stem

½ cup pigeon peas/thuvar dal

1½ tbsps tamarind sauce

¾ tsp sambar powder

¼ tsp turmeric powder

¼ cup coconut,

ground 6 curry

leaves

½ tsp salt

For Seasoning:

¼ tsp mustard seeds

½ tsp husked split dark gram/urad dal

¼ tsp asafetida/hing

powder 2 tsps oil

Method:

1. Cook the pigeon peas in 2½ cups of water to a delicate consistency. Then again, pressure cook for a whistle, lower fire and cook for 10 minutes. Switch off the fire. At the point when the strain diminishes totally open and use.

2. Wash vegetable in running water and cook in two cups of water with the sambar powder, turmeric powder and salt. Cover and stew for 8 - 10 minutes over medium hotness or until done.

3. Add the tamarind sauce, salt and the cooked lentil and keep on cooking for a few minutes.

4. Heat the oil, pop the mustard and delicately brown the dark gram. Add asafetida and dish the ground coconut for a large portion of a moment or until a dim brilliant in color.

5. Wet and smash curry leaves, sauté and add to the bubbling kootu. Stew for 40 seconds. Add a quarter cup water if excessively thick and heat to the point of boiling for a minute.

6. Serve as a principle course.

BANANA STEM IN BLENDED COCONUT YOGURT

vazhathandu mor kootu

Prep Time: 12-14 mins. Serves 3 portions

Banana Stem in Blended Coconut Yogurt

Ingredients:

7-8" long banana stem

2 cups yogurt, beaten with ¾ cup

water 6 curry leaves

½ tsp salt

For Seasoning:

¼ tsp mustard

seeds 1 tsp oil

For The Paste:

1 tbsp rice

1 cup coconut,

ground/frozen 2 green

chillis

Method:

1. Soak rice in steaming hot water for 20 minutes and mix with coconut and green chillis into a fine paste.

2. Wash the slashed vegetable in running water, channel and quickly cook in some salted water. Cover and stew over a medium fire for 4-5 minutes. On the other hand, pressure cook for a whistle. Whenever the strain decreases totally, open and use.

3. Add the yogurt and mixed glue to the steamed vegetable

4. In a little pot, heat the oil, pop the mustard, sauté the wet squashed curry leaves.

5. Simmer over medium hotness until it thickens lightly.

6. Serve with steamed rice.

Tasty Tip: Top the dish with half a teaspoon of coconut oil for extra flavor.

RIPE BANANAS

vazhapazham/ kela

The ready banana has a significant influence in the strict, social and culinary existences of the Tamilians. The banana is offered, alongside four betel leaves and betel nuts, to the Gods in sanctuaries, in strict services and in the every day pujas at home.

Today, clinical examination credits characteristics to the banana that were well established realities to our people of yore. In wedding functions, the wedding couple are taken care of with banana and milk. At the point when another lady enters her better half's home, she is given banana cuts in milk as the principal thing to eat. A banana can assist with normalizing the heartbeat, send oxygen to the mind and direct the body's water balance. It assists with pressure, which raises potassium levels, and serves to re-total the metabolism.

Bananas contain potassium, called "the salt of insight". It supports learning capacities and makes understudies more ready. The organic product neutralizes over-causticity and diminishes bothering by covering the coating of the stomach, particularly after a weighty dinner. Subsequently, in the Indian setting, it would be savvier to say "A banana daily keeps the specialist away!"

There are numerous assortments of ready bananas accessible in various nations. The nendra pazham is a long, yellow assortment from Kerala that has a fine surface and is great for cooking sweet dishes and sticks/jellies.
Other yellow assortments can be substituted.

RIPE BANANA RELISH

nendhra pazha varati

Prep Time: 10 mins. Makes 1 liter

The Palghat Tamil version of the jam/ jelly.

Ingredients:

4 - 5 bananas

¼ lb jaggery/gur or palm

sugar 4 tbsps explained

margarine/ghee

Method:

1. Heat some water and mix in the jaggery. Strain to eliminate rubbish, empty it back into the skillet and cook for five minutes until the blend accomplishes a remedy surface. Keep this aside.

2. Peel and quarter the bananas and make them into little pieces. Mix in a tablespoon of dissolved ghee for a couple of moments shutting top every so often until it gets to a delicate mash.

3. Blend and add to the jaggery combination. Gather the ghee and blend them all into a single unit. Mix for two additional minutes. Eliminate and serve fresh.

Timely Tip: Store in an airtight container and refrigerate. Most flavorful and filling, this banana is a specialty in Kerala cuisine. You can substitute any large yellow variety of banana to prepare this dish.

Chakka Varati - Banana Jam

RIPE BANANA IN JAGGERY SAUCE

chenda muriyan

Ripe banana in jaggery sauce

Prep Time: 5 mins. Makes ½ kilo

'Chenda Muriyan' is the name given for this dish in Malayalam. The Palghat Brahmins are ingenious in making a dish tastier and better. This one was often prepared by my maternal grandmom. No compromise was made on the ingredients. It was an insult to the dish itself. Generally it was grown in the backyard of a home.

Ingredients:

3 - 4 over-ready bananas (nendram variety)

¼ lb jaggery/gur or palm

sugar 2 tbsps explained

margarine/ghee

Method:

1. Peel the banana and cut them up. Mix over a medium fire for 2 to 3 minutes adding a spot of ghee. At the point when the blended smell of the ghee and the matured organic product rises, switch it off. Heat some water and mix in the jaggery. Strain to eliminate filth, empty it back into the skillet and cook for five minutes until the blend accomplishes a remedy texture.

2. Now add and tenderly blend in the remainder of the ghee to give it a decent blend. A kind of ghee, jaggery and the banana blended across the board - tastes heavenly!

Timely Tip: Have it fresh and store it for not more than a day. These dishes are old gems in a Kerala home. Pretty easy to prepare.

I say it again as I have depicted in the last page of my book - 'develop your own vegetables at home'. No patio? Don't sweat it - in green sacks and pots. My nursery master Jameela Ahmed develops her banana tree in a barrel. Do be determined and patient and your discipline comes automatically.

JACKFRUIT

palapazham/ khatal

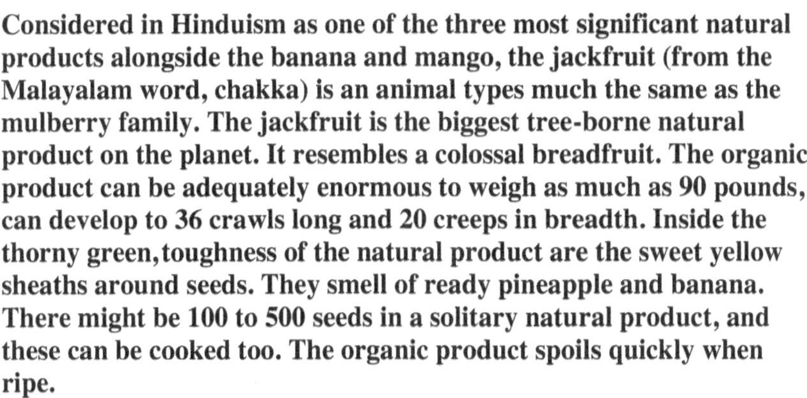

Considered in Hinduism as one of the three most significant natural products alongside the banana and mango, the jackfruit (from the Malayalam word, chakka) is an animal types much the same as the mulberry family. The jackfruit is the biggest tree-borne natural product on the planet. It resembles a colossal breadfruit. The organic product can be adequately enormous to weigh as much as 90 pounds, can develop to 36 crawls long and 20 creeps in breadth. Inside the thorny green, toughness of the natural product are the sweet yellow sheaths around seeds. They smell of ready pineapple and banana. There might be 100 to 500 seeds in a solitary natural product, and these can be cooked too. The organic product spoils quickly when ripe.

There are two primary assortments a stringy, delicate, soft assortment and another that has fresh and crunchy organic products. The crude organic product is cooked as well.

PREPARATION TIPS

a. Oil the hands with coconut oil prior to setting up the jackfruit.

b. The natural product inside the skin is a white mass that gives out a smooth, tacky sap.

c. Cut the top of the natural product, split and quarter it to uncover the inside.

d. With a sharp blade, edge out each yellow fruit.

e. Slice and eliminate the seed and another skin that covers the seed.

f. Dry the seeds before you use them and eliminate the earthy colored layer that covers them.

Shanthi, my lovely kitchen mate going through the
different strides of cutting a local jackfruit.

JACKFRUIT KARI

chakka kari

Prep Time: 15 mins. Serves 3 portions

The raw fruit can be cooked into a stir-fry or a curry.

Ingredients:

20 pieces crude jackfruit

8 - 10 jackfruit seeds,

delicate 3 tbsps coconut,

grated

2 tbsps curry leaves

¼ tsp turmeric powder

½ tsp bean stew powder, optional

½ tsp earthy colored sugar/sugar

½ tsp salt

For The Paste:

1 dried red chilli

3 tbsps coconut,

ground 1 tbsp cumin

seeds

Roast the bean stew in a little oil and mix until firm and red.

Coarsely pound every one of the flavors and keep aside.

For Seasoning:

¼ tsp mustard seeds

½ tsp split husked dark gram/urad dal

1 tsp oil

Method:

1. Grease the palm with oil and scoop out the fruit.

2. Deseed and afterward hack the organic product mash and the seeds into little pieces or coarsely squash them.

3. Heat oil in a profound skillet, pop the mustard seeds and brown the dark gram. Add some water with salt and boil.

4. Add the cleaved seeds and mash, turmeric powder and close the dish with a top and steam over a medium fire for four to five minutes. Then again, pressure-cook for one whistle.

5. Open top and mix for a couple of moments until delicate. Add wet squashed curry leaves, the coarsely beat flavors, earthy colored sugar, bean stew powder/cayenne pepper and salt if required.

6. Stir in the ground coconut and eliminate from flame.

JACKFRUIT FUDGE
chakka varati

Prep Time: 15 mins. serves 3 portions

A delicious sweet dish that can be used as a sweet chutney, jam or preserve or just eaten plain! It tastes heavenly.

Ingredients:

2½ cups ready jackfruit, cleaved

fine 1 cup jaggery/brown sugar

4 tbsps explained margarine/ghee

Method:

1. Rub oil in the palms and cut the jackfruit in the middle with a sharp meat knife.

2. Scoop the natural product from within and eliminate the seed.

3. Stir the jackfruit in a tablespoon until it turns soft and delicate. This cycle requires a couple of moments when you mix close cover a few times.

4. Add a quarter cup of water to jaggery and liquefy over a low fire. Strain to eliminate the scum.

5. In a profound pot add the jaggery fluid and mixed jackfruit and mix over a low fire for seven minutes or until it thickens into a fudge.

6. Add the remainder of the ghee blend, and eliminate from flame.

7. Cool, fill a compartment with a firm cover and refrigerate.

Timely Tip: If using brown sugar, you may add it to the blended jackfruit and stir until it turns into fudge. Add the ghee mix together and remove from flame.

Makes extraordinary spread for sandwiches! Substitute ready bananas on the off chance that jackfruit isn't accessible. The bananas can be crushed without bubbling and cooked with jaggery and coconut milk.

Refer to the chakka pradhamam or jackfruit pudding formula in my book, 'Samayal'.

FRUITS IN SYRUP- THE HEAVENLY NECTAR

panchamrutam

Prep Time: 15 mins. Serves 4 portions

**Known as Palani panchamrutam, or the five nectar delight, this syrup is offered to Lord Muruga in his temple atop the Palani hills in Tamil Nadu.
When we talk about
nectar/amrutham, be guaranteed it has a genuinely heavenly taste.**

Fruits in Syrup-the Heavenly Nectar

Ingredients:
5 huge ready bananas

½lb dates, deseeded

½lb raisins, crushed

¼lb cashew nuts, broken

little 1 cup powdered

jaggery/gur

½lb honey

¼lb sugar sweets bits/karkandu

½ tsp cardamom, powdered coarsely with skin

Method:

1. Peel, cut and quarter the bananas.

2. Chop the dates into bit sizes.

3. Heat 1½ cups of water in an enormous container and mix in the jaggery. Add the bananas, raisins, dates and broken cashew bits. Mix for four to five minutes until it thickens a little. It gets thicker when it cools.

4. Add squashed cardamom, mix briefly and afterward add honey. At the point when somewhat cooled, add the sugar and candy bits and mix.

5. Serve cooled.

Tasty tip: The pancha in panchamrutham refers to the five nectars that go into it. Fruits like papaya, melon and grapefruit cannot be used. To give texture to the fruit mash, fine sugar candy bits/ karkandu is traditionally used.

CONVALESCENCE MEAL

pathiya saapadu

Treatment for actual issues started with diet limitations in the home. One hypothesis said, langanam parama aushadam signifying, "Doing without food is the best medication for any sickness." The option was to eat a dinner with boring and effectively absorbable dishes. One more specially was to ceremonially clean the stomach related framework with a portion of castor oil that cleansed the stomach. This portion was directed routinely to the entire family.

The supper that was served after this cleanse was called pathiya-saapadu. Individuals experiencing fevers, hacks and colds and ladies after the conveyance of a youngster (for 40 days) were totally served these exceptionally pre-arranged dishes that went to make improvement meals.

SPICY PEPPERCORN RICE

milagu sadham

Prep Time: 8 mins. Serves 4 portions

Spicy Peppercorn Rice

Ingredients:

1 cup rice

6 curry leaves

½ tsp salt

Collect In A bowl For The Paste:

1½ tsps peppercorn

1 tbsp bengal gram/chana dal

1 red chilli

½ tsp asafetida/hing

powder 1 tsp explained

spread/ghee

Roast flavors for a couple of moments until the

fragrance rises. Powder fine and keep aside.

For Seasoning:

½ tsps mustard seeds

2 tbsps explained margarine/ghee

Method:

1. Cook rice in 2½ cups of water and keep to the side. Guarantee it is cooked to a grainy surface for mixing.

2. Heat the ghee and pop the mustard.

3. Add the popped mustard, wet and squashed curry leaves and the powder to the rice and blend delicately and well. A few add the remainder of the ghee and present with toasted papads/popadams.

4. Place the papad/popadam in a microwave and toast for two minutes. At the point when it puffs up, eliminate and present with pepper rice.

TOASTED PEPPER IN TAMARIND SAUCE

milagu kuzhambu

Prep Time: 10 mins. Serves 4 portions

Toasted Pepper in Tamarind Sauce

Ingredients:

2 tbsps tamarind purée ¼ tsp mustard

seeds 6 curry leaves

1 tsp explained spread/ghee

½ tsp

salt 1

tsp oil

Collect In A Bowl For The Paste:

1½   tsps

peppercorn   1

tbsp   bengal

gram   1   tbsp

cumin seeds

1 tbsp coriander seeds

¼ tsp asafetida/hing powder

Method:

1. Heat the oil and meal the flavors for the glue on a low fire briefly.
Mix into a fine glue, adding a little water.

2. Heat the ghee and pop the mustard. Add the tamarind sauce, glue and
salt and mix well. Add some water, cover and stew over medium hotness
for 10 minutes, blending sometimes until it thickens to a remedy
consistency.

3. Add wet and squashed curry leaves and mix for 15 seconds and
eliminate from flame.

4. Some homes use drumsticks in this sauce for added flavor.

LENTIL CHUTNEY

paruppu thuvayal

Prep Time: 8 mins. Serves 3 portions

Ingredients:

½ cup pigeon peas/thuvar dal

1 red chilli

3 tbsps ground coconut

½ tsp asafetida/hing

powder 4 curry leaves

¼ tsp

salt 1

tsp oil

Method:

1. Heat the oil and mix the pigeon peas briefly until light brilliant in
shading. Add the bean stew and asafetida and mix for 10 seconds.

2. Now add wet squashed curry leaves and combine it as one. Mix into a
thick glue with salt and coconut utilizing a tablespoon of water.

STIR FRIED CURRIED POWDER

angaaya podi

Prep Time: 5 mins. Serves 3 portions

This is a healthy and flavorful powder. This powder was served to help digestion. If you do not have stone salt at home, substitute one teaspoon table salt instead.

Ingredients:

½ cup cumin

½ cup turkey berry

½ cup dark nightshade

berries 20 curry leaves

½ tsp asafetida/hing

powder 1 tsp dried ginger

powder

½ tsp pepper

1½ tsp ocean

salt

1 tsp explained margarine/ghee

Method:

1. Melt the ghee, mixing in the turkey berry, dark nightshade, curry leaves, cumin, pepper and asafetida for a minute.

2. Blend these, ginger powder, and the ocean salt into a fine powder and use.

3. Mix with hot steamed rice and a dab of dissolved ghee.

CURRY SAUCE

ericha kuzhambu

Prep Time: 10 mins. Serves 4 portions

Curry Sauce

No refrigerators and a hot tropical environment, combined with a naturally frugal nature that believed in not wasting food, made the Tamil housewife very innovative indeed. Thus, when the day's food was left over, it was all combined—the dry vegetables, the wet kootus, sambars and rasams and recycled into a new dish called ericha kuzhambu. You could use onions in this dish.

Method:

1. In a profound wok, add two tablespoons of until oil and season with mustard seeds and curry leaves and some stripped and cleaved shallots.

2. Pour in every one of the extras other than yogurt based dishes-and let them simmer.

3. Let all the water vanish, leaving behind a pale mass.

4. This thick glue/chutney can be utilized as a side dish with curd rice.

SAMARADHANAI VIRUNDHU

All our celebrations used to be connected to the community. A village was usually made up of about 300 people and the surrounding villages or communities were connected to each other through marriages and family ties. The communities were brought together when there were family occasions and temple festivities. The 1500 strong community of the area came together, contributed in kind and service to celebrate such events.

This solid local area feeling was the premise of their security and individuals shared their normal advantages and objectives. An event was deficient on the off chance that a 3 course supper was not served to the participants.

This is a typical dinner that is intended for all-sama importance equivalent, aradhanai meaning petition, honor or love. The entire town or local area would consolidate to cook, serve and eat this conventional feast on banana leaves in pandis - lines of individuals who sat on the floor. Everyone would sit and eat together in a typical pandal or cover covered space with open sides that let the cool wind stream through.

Back then, travel was not something simple to embrace. The vast majority had Tirupathi as the kuladeivam (family god) or had commitments to families they imparted prime loyalties to. They were committed to visit their sanctuary in some measure one time each year, particularly as a thanksgiving signal.

The course to Tirupathi was extreme slope landscape, and you needed to make a trip by bullock truck to the foundation of the slopes and afterward move up the seven hills.

Likewise, individuals additionally went on journey to far away places, and their return was an event for incredible delight and thanksgiving. A celebratory feast virundu sappadu-was served to family and friends.

Many families played out the samaradhanai puja to Venkatachalapathy or Lord Balaji once every year on a Saturday in the long stretch of Puratasi on the Tamil schedule (September - October). Couples were respected with a bubbly dinner and given sesame. Rice was made in huge amounts and was offered to brahmacharis or unmarried young men who wore the hallowed string in the neighborhood.

In the image above on the right, the Lord comes to the earth as a rancher to plant seeds all at once of dry season. A few families likewise played out this samaradhanai to Lord Muruga subsequent to playing out a unique puja called thirukalyanam. A few travelers embraced a thorough quick for a couple of days to visit every one of the six holy places of Muruga-aarupadai veedu-and the samaradhanai feast was effectively broken this quick. Anyway attractive a gift, the recipient could have aching for some more. On this event when such a supper was served the favors given were in overflow. The photos here are great: a painting and a figure of the marriage of the Lord and his consort.

The visitors were invited generously with cries of "Vango, vango" (welcome, welcome) and were regarded with sandalwood glue and kumkumam (vermilion), with a sprinkling of rose water as they showed up for the occasion.

The samaradhanai supper is an adaptable one and not limited to specific vegetables or dishes. The menu was conventional as befitted a 3 course meal

The wood apple includes normally in Tamil cooking. The natural product was tried for readiness when it turned out to be light in weight and skiped off the floor like a ball. Then the hard shell was broken and the pulp mixed and coarsely ground with jaggery and seasoned with a little cardamom powder. This should likewise be possible in the conventional ammi. The sweet, woody, somewhat tart taste had the public licking their fingers in delight.
The hard shell of the wood apple was not discarded, however added to the rasam to improve its flavor.

Three natural products are related with a happy or custom supper in the Tamil menu. Once more, these were natural products accessible effectively in the plantations or patios of families and homes. They were mango, jackfruit and

banana. For samaradanai dinners, individuals, sharing the local area soul, would liberally give natural product from their own stock alongside rice, grams, lentils, tamarind and vegetables. The sweet laddoo, that resembles a ball is otherwise called kunjaa laadu in some Tamil speech. This would have begun from the word gunjaa laddoo, as the Sanskrit word gunjaa implies berry. This berry was utilized as a proportion of weight, particularly for gold. Since a laddu, a firmly pressed circle of numerous boondis or beads of singed gram flour, it resembled a minuscule berry, consequently it became kunja laddoo.

NOTE

The recipes given in this section can easily serve four people.

The food is completely cooked new upon the arrival of the blowout. As in every strict feast, the food is served untasted all of the time to guests.

A spoonful of salt is served on the left corner of the banana leaf to compensate for individual preferences. The plans given underneath could be for 3 individuals. You need to add on segments for more people.

The order of recipes featured in this section follows the custom of serving the dishes in a particular order on the banana leaf for special occasions. A pair of paruppu thengai cones, representing the male and female concept is part of any important function like marriages, ceremonies related to pregnancy, birth, sacred thread ceremony, etc. I have timed though not quantified these dishes as they are prepared for a feast. You could always use the remaining the next day.

The four-holder dish (displayed above left) was for the most part utilized for a dining experience when a huge social affair of individuals were served. It was emblematic, it was advantageous and through and through an incredible idea.

The Paruppu-thengai koodu (above right) is an extremely customary tapered pair of desserts arranged during favorable events and for weddings. Various types of conelike molded desserts were made for various events and they had an enlivening covering (as the one above) uncommonly made or purchased to give it a stylish look.

TRADITIONAL RICE COCONUT DESSERT

idichu pizhinja payasam

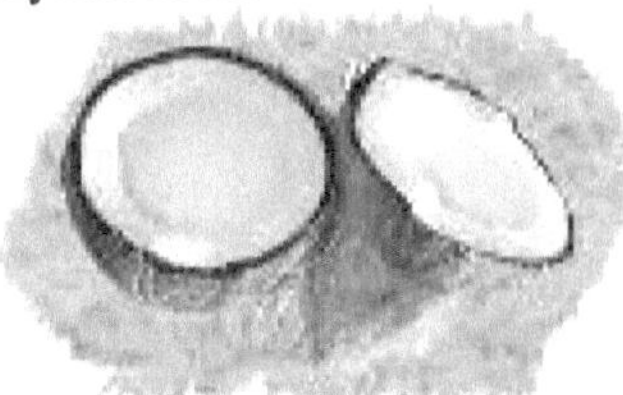

This is a sweet dish served first on the banana leaf for a festive meal.

Traditional Rice Coconut Dessert

Ingredients:

1 cup molasses/jaggery/gur

½ cup water

1 cup coconut

milk 1 cup milk

2 tbsps cashew nuts, broken

½ tsp cardamom,

powdered 1 tsp explained

margarine/ghee

For The Paste:

2 tbsps rice

4 tbsps ground coconut

Method:

1. Soak the rice in steaming hot water for 10 minutes and mix finely with the coconut. Mix this over a low fire for five minutes until completely cooked. Keep aside.

2. Mix the mixed glue into the milk without lumps.

3. In a profound non-stick container, heat the water to dissolve the jaggery. Strain to eliminate rubbish and keep aside.

4. Roast the cashew nuts in ghee for 15 seconds until brilliant brown in shading. Keep aside.

5. Add the glue to the softened jaggery and mix over a medium fire for two minutes. Add the coconut milk and cardamom, mixed cooked rice and coconut to this combination and mix for two minutes.

6. Remove from fire and embellishment with the broiled cashew nuts.

GINGER COCONUT YOGURT

inji thengai thayir pachadi

Ingredients:

2 cups yogurt, beaten

¼ tsp mustard

seeds 3 curry

leaves

1 tsp oil

¼ tsp salt

For The Paste:

2" piece of ginger, peeled

2 tbsps coconut, ground/frozen

Method:

1. Blend the ginger and coconut into a coarse paste.

2. Heat the oil and pop the mustard. Eliminate from fire and add the wet and squashed curry leaves and salt.

3. Add this with mixed glue to the yogurt and blend well.

Tasty Tip: This spiced yoghurt preparation has an amazing taste and flavor! Tamil food rocks.

SWEET SOUR MANGO RELISH

manga pachadi

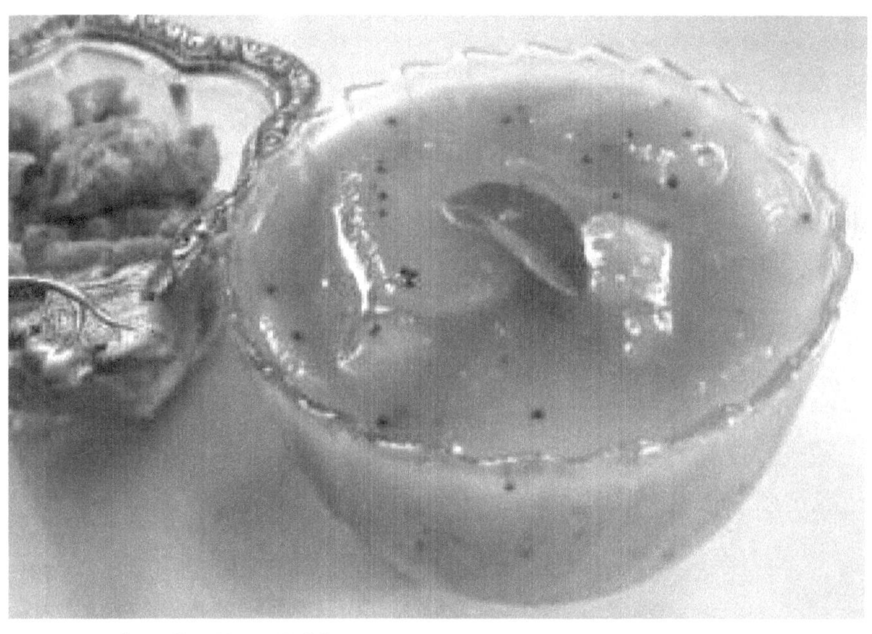

Sweet Sour Mango Relish

Color, subtlety and traditional habits come to the fore and one such dish is the 'mangai pachadi'. Generally neem flowers stir-fried in ghee is

added to the final pachadi. Hence this sauce significantly denotes – the sweetness bitterness and sourness that is part of our transient life on this earth!

Ingredients:

1 huge crude mango

½ cup jaggery/brown sugar

¼ tsp mustard seeds

1 tsp oil

Method:

1. Peel the mango's skin totally as it cooks better. Cut the mango into slim lopsided pieces. The more firm, crude and tart the mango, the better the dish.

2. Melt the jaggery in quarter cup of water over a medium fire and strain to eliminate filth. Keep aside.

3. In a pot, heat the oil and pop the mustard. Add the mango cuts and mix delicately for 30 seconds. Add a large portion of some water, cover and stew over medium hotness. Require off the top following two or three minutes and cook until delicate however firm.

4. Add the jaggery and mix. Permit to stew for 40 seconds or until it thickens like a sauce.

Timely Tip: If the mango is sour, add more jaggery. Jaggery powder is available in all the Indian groceries. It can be added directly to the sour cooked mango.

A semi-ready mango can likewise be made into a pachadi. This dish has a prepared taste special to this community.

SNAKE GOURD IN LENTIL CRUMBLE

pudalangai usili

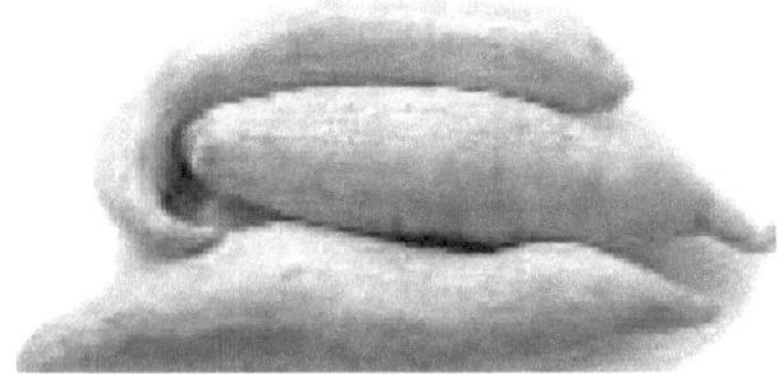

Snake Gourd in Lentil Crumble

Ingredients:

1 lb snake gourd

½ tsp salt

For The Usili:

½ cup pigeon peas/thuvar dal

3 dried red chillis

¾ tsp asafetida powder

¼ tsp turmeric

powder 8 curry

leaves

½ tsp salt

Cover the pigeon peas in enough hot water to cover them completely and drench for around 10 to 20 minutes.

Blend this coarsely alongside the other ingredients.

Steam for around 20 minutes in a rice cooker or straighten the usili and zap in the microwave for 2-3 minutes.

Insert a wooden pick/fork; when it confesses all it is

finished. Cool the steamed lentil and disintegrate without

lumps.

For Seasoning:

¼ tsp mustard seeds

½ cup sesame oil/oil

Method:

1. Slit the vegetable, deseed and slash into little pieces.

2. Heat a large portion of some water in a profound skillet with salt and add the cleaved snake gourd. Throw softly with a spatula until rich green in color.

3. Over a medium fire, cover and cook for two minutes. Open the dish and sauté until delicate however firm. Keep aside.

4. Heat the oil and pop the mustard. Presently add the usili combination; wet and squash a large portion of the curry leaves.

5. Stir well for three minutes. Into this, add the cooked vegetable and wet squashed curry leaves and mix delicately briefly over medium hotness until soft

and crumbly.

FRESH GREEN BANANA STIR FRY

vazhakai pachai kari

Very simple but most flavorful to prepare, this stir-fried kari with light spices is a huge hit in Tamil homes.

Fresh Green Banana Stir Fry

Ingredients:

2 medium-sized green bananas

½ tsp turmeric powder

¼ tsp asafetida/hing powder

A spot of squashed red

pepper 5 curry leaves

½ tsp salt

For Seasoning:

¼ tsp mustard seeds

2 dried red chillis, split

2 tbsps oil

Method:

1. Peel the banana. Quarter it and absorb water to stay away from discoloring.

2. In a profound non-stick container, heat the oil, pop the mustard and dish the dried red chillis.

3. Drain water and add the banana, mixing in the turmeric powder. Close cover for 30 - 40 seconds. Open cover and mix in the asafetida powder. Add a teaspoon a greater amount of oil if too dry.

4. Wet and smash the curry leaves, add them and eliminate the dish from the flame.

5. Serve this yummy sound dish as a side to a principle course.

CRISPY JAGGERY FUDGE

manoharam paruppu thengai

The cones of sweet savories are an important part of any function. They represent the male and female aspect of family life.

Ingredients:

10 cups rice

2½ cups husked split green gram/moong dal

¾ cup bengal gram/chana dal

2 cups jaggery/gur

1 cup unsalted spread, room temperature

¼ cup

salt Oil

for frying

Method:

1. Keep the murukku/chakli producer helpful and brush its internal parts with oil.

2. Mix the dals and meal on a medium fire for two minutes or until there is a particular aroma.

3. Blend into a fine powder alongside the rice. Sifter it fine and set aside.

4. Divide the flour blend into three parts. Set up the batter not long prior to broiling, since it can solidify inside a couple of moments and the shade of the sev will darken.

5. Soften the margarine and gap into three portions.

6. Dissolve the salt in three cups of heated water and separation this too into three bits. Blend one piece every one of the spread, water and flour and make the batter sufficiently delicate to go through the murukku press and plate easily.

7. While this is being done, heat the oil in a wok over a medium fire for profound searing. Bring down the flame.

8. Take the metal circle with the adjusted example and spot it at the lower part of the press. Fill the batter in the upper cavity. Press out the mixture in little roundabout developments on a lubed plate. Slide this plate tenderly into the stewing oil.

9. Shortly, the batter will sneak off the plate. With an opened spoon, turn the sev tenderly so they don't remain together. Fry until they are light brilliant all over.

10. Drain and drop the murukkus on to a kitchen towel to deplete off abundance oil.

11. Repeat this cycle utilizing three to four lubed plates. Go through the excess fixings and set up the mixture once more for each batch.

12. Roughly break the murukku and keep aside.

13. Heat 1½ cups of water and soften the jaggery. Strain to eliminate filth and

return the syrup to the fire. Mix consistently for 8 - 10 minutes until it thickens into syrup.

14. Check the consistency of the syrup by dropping a little bead into a large portion of some water. It ought not break up in water and you ought to have the option to fold it into a minuscule globule. Whenever you toss it back into the water it should make a "ping" sound.

15. Take off the fire and right away void the murukku into the quite hot jaggery syrup. Blend well until the murukku incorporates into the syrup.

16. Grease the cones with the ghee and empty the hot combination into them.

Tasty Tip: After the puja was over the paruppu thengai pair was given to the son-in-law of the family as an honor. It is broken up, distributed and eaten at tiffin/ snack time.

Chakli Maker: Indian Noodle Press

Murukku/chakli producers made of metal and aluminum are accessible in Indian stores. These machines have 5 to 6 metal plates with holes in various designs.

Iron vegetable shaper, wok with holds (alluded to as kaadhu (ears), and a scoop utilized in conventional homes. Wood flames and coal fires are as yet utilized in customary homes in towns. Dried cow fertilizer cakes are likewise used to get fires going for cooking. Every one of these eco-accommodating propensities have existed in India for centuries.

BUTTER PEPPER CRUNCHIES

karaa sevai

Butter Pepper Crunchies

Ingredients:

5 cups rice

1¾ cups husked split dark gram/urad dal

¾ cup bengal gram/chana dal

¼ lb unsalted margarine at room temperature

½ tsp dark pepper, coarsely powdered

¼ tsp asafetida/hing powder

½ - ¾ tsp

salt Oil for

searing

Method:

1. In a profound non-stick skillet, dry meal both dark gram and bengal gram on a medium fire for 3 - 4 minutes until an unmistakable fragrance rises.

2. Blend into a flour alongside the rice. Sifter the flour fine and set aside.

3. Add the pepper, asafetida to the flour partition it into three segments. Set up the mixture not long prior to broiling as it can solidify inside a couple of moments and the shade of the sev will darken.

4. Soften the margarine and separation into three portions.

5. Dissolve the salt in three cups of high temp water and gap this too into three portions.

6. Mix one part every one of the spread, water and flour and make the batter adequately delicate to go through the murukku/chakli press.

7. Meanwhile, heat the oil in a profound wok over a medium fire. Bring down the flame.

8. Take the metal plate with adjusted openings and spot it at the lower part of the press. Fill the mixture in the upper cavity and press it out in sprays so that main half-inch bits of the sev fall straightforwardly into the stewing oil.

9. With an opened scoop, turn the kara sevai around so the pieces don't stay together. Fry until they are light brilliant all over.

10. Drain and put the crunchies on a kitchen paper to eliminate overabundance oil.

11. Repeat this cycle and utilize the leftover segments of fixings. Make sure to set up the mixture once more for each batch.

FRIED GRAM SUGAR DROPLETS

kunja laddoo

Fried Gram Sugar Droplets

Ingredients:

2½ cups bengal gram flour/besan

2 cups sugar

2 tbsps cashew nuts,

split 1 tsp squashed

cardamom

A couple of strands of saffron
1 tsp explained spread/ghee

Oil for frying

Method:

1. Roast the cashew nuts in ghee until golden.

2. Add 1½ cups water to the bengal gram flour/besan and blend well to make a slim player of dropping consistency.

3. Heat the oil and drop a ladleful of hitter through an opened spoon/scoop with adjusted, pea-size openings. This scoop is a sunken, to hold the mixture as it fails to work out. Inside the space of seconds the boondhis are done and consistently crispy.

4. Mash the saffron in a little hot milk until the milk turns a profound orange.

5. In a profound pan, add some water to the sugar and mix until it becomes syrup of one-string consistency. Remove the flame.

6. Add the saffron fluid and cardamom. Set aside.

7. Add these boondhis to the sugar syrup. Add the seared cashew nuts and squashed cardamom and blend well. (Cardamom powder is home made. Continuously pound or powder cardamom with skin.)

8. Grease your palms with ghee and form the sweet boondhis into firm golf-sized balls. Cool and store in a sealed shut container.

Timely Tip: This can be made the previous day. If you desire to serve something made fresh on the same day, substitute with a rava kesari (semolina dessert). Semolina dessert is described in my book, 'Samayal'.

TAMARIND RICE

puliyodharai

Tamarind Rice

Ingredients:

1 cup rice

3 tbsps tamarind sauce

¼ tsp turmeric powder

½ tsp asafetida/hing powder

½ cup simmered peanuts, skinned

½ cup sesame oil or any

oil 2 teaspoons salt

For Seasoning:

¼ tsp mustard seeds

½ tsp bengal gram

4 dried red chillis,

divided 8 curry leaves

Method:

1. Cook the rice in five cups of water. Each grain of the cooked rice should be discrete. Put away to cool.

2. Heat a tablespoon of oil, pop the mustard and brown the gram. Add the chillis and mix until a splendid shading. Add the peanuts and sauté for 20 seconds. Presently a tad bit of the curry leaves.

3. Add the tamarind mash, some water, the turmeric powder, asafetida powder and salt. Cover and stew over a medium fire for three minutes.

4. Open the top and cook until it turns into a thick sauce - a remedy consistency.

5. Add the excess oil. Wet the remainder of the curry leaves smash them in your palm and add. Take it off the stove.

6. This is called pulikaachal, which goes to make puliyodharai rice (called so whenever it is blended in with steamed rice). Blend the sauce into the rice without squashing it.

Tasty Tip: Add half a teaspoon of jaggery to balance the hot and tangy flavor of the tamarind rice. For most South Indian traditional dishes, sesame oil is used, adding a special flavor.

SLICED YAM CHIP/ WAFERS

chenaikizhangu varuval

Ingredients:

1 lb yam

1 tsp cayenne pepper/stew

powder 1 tsp asafetida/hing

powder

2 tsps salt
2 cups oil for profound frying

Method:

1. Remove the thick, mottled tanish skin of the sweet potato. Wash completely and cut the sweet potato with a chips slicer. Submerge the pieces in cold water.

2. Heat two cups of water. Channel the sweet potato and add to this bubbling water. Permit to stew for 30 seconds. Eliminate and wipe the whitened vegetable with a dry cloth.

3. Heat two cups of oil in a profound wok until it arrives at the phase of smoking up. Lower fire and add the sweet potato pieces. Delicately turn over the chips so they fry equitably. Each time you add a new clump to sear, guarantee the oil temperature is maintained.

4. Line a plate with a paper towel, put the chips on it so it assimilates the overabundance oil.

5. Now sprinkle a combination of salt, stew powder and asafetida powder on it and stir it up. Store in an impenetrable canister.

STEAMED RICE IN A TAMIL HOME

Rice can be cooked in many ways: directly in a pan of water, with the remaining water being drained off at the end; in a pressure-cooker/pan; in a rice-cooker; or in a microwave. Down south, the ideal consistency of steamed rice is considered to be a light fluffy grain like the petals of a jasmine flower.

A rice-cooker accompanies an internal dish. Add 2½ cups of water in the internal dish and press some lemon or lime juice to forestall its obscuring during the steaming system. Keep the washed rice with the expected water in one more metallic dish and spot it in the rice-cooker, in the midst of the water in the cooker. Steamed rice cooked this way is soft and grainy, rather than rice set straightforwardly in a rice-cooker. The explanation is that rice cooked straightforwardly in a rice cooker begins getting papery and hard in the event that not polished off immediately.

Generally, rice ought not be soft or excessively dry; the water estimation is a half cup something else for old rice. Standard estimation for South Indian rice is 3 to 3½ cups of water to one cup of rice. Matured rice is liked to new rice.

In a Tamil home, steamed rice is served for the principal course, with cooked and softly salted pigeon peas and a dab of ghee.

A tension cooker/skillet saves time and holds the shading and kind of the different fixings. Aside from a skillet or a pan, vegetables, sambars, kuzhambus and kootus can be straightforwardly ready in the strain cooker or container. Cooking in a strain cookers or dish is portrayed in the part, "Significant Tips" given toward the start of the book.

PREPARING YOGURT AT HOME

During circumstances such as the present, business yogurt is produced using new, sanitized and homogenized cow's milk under painstakingly controlled temperatures and brooding circumstances. At times, business yogurt is purified after the way of life has been added. This stretches the time span of usability. but it ends up killing the healthy bacteria present in the yogurt. These microorganisms really assist with combatting acid reflux in the stomach or digestion tracts. A definitive outcome is that yogurt handled this way demonstrates useless in accomplishing this end. But preparing yogurt at home is infinitely simpler, and of course, healthier. It is significantly less expensive, as well; one has complete command over the newness, the nature of fixings utilized, the flavor and the calorie content.

Home-made yogurt enjoys an upper hand over business yogurt in the sense one can control the taste as indicated by private inclination. You can either decide the level of pungency by changing the hatching period. This has a tremendous effect, as it empowers the fulfillment of innovative action in the kitchen. Nonetheless, flavor and consistency will vary with the sort of milk used to make the yogurt. While heating up the new milk, mix often to guarantee no skin is shaped on the

surface.
This skin removes important protein from the yogurt. In the event that the skin structures, eliminate it with a spatula. Presently permit the completely bubbled milk to cool for around 12 - 14 minutes. It should in any case be more than warm-practically hot. Now, add one to two tablespoons of beaten yogurt to the bubbled milk. Utilize a wooden or steel hand churner and work it till the milk froths at the top.

The simplest method for keeping a consistent temperature during the hatching time frame is to guarantee the milk is put in a dish with a shut cover in a lit broiler for around 4 to 4½ hours. Some of the time, in colder spots, it functions admirably when set in a preheated stove at 120 degrees with the pilot light on. This guarantees the pilot light offers sufficient warmth.

Alternatively, place a skillet of boiling water in the base rack of the stove. This ought to get the job done. In a warm tropical spot like South India, simply adding the starter to more-than-warm milk and keeping it outside for a couple of hours in the kitchen is adequate to deliver great hand crafted yogurt.

Yogurt can be mixed into pungent or sweet smoothies, lassi or buttermilk.

STIR FRIED OKRA SIMMERED IN YOGURT

vendakkai mor kuzhambu

Browning and adding the okra to a dish adds a traditional flavor to any Tamil dish.

Stir Fried Okra Simmered in Yogurt

Ingredients:

14-16 okras

2 cups of yogurt, beaten in ½ some water

¼ tsp asafetida/hing

powder 6 curry leaves

½ tsp

salt 2

tbsps oil

For Seasoning:

¼ tsp mustard

seeds 1 tsp oil

For The Paste:

1½ tbsps rice

¾ cup coconut, grated

¼ tsp mustard seeds

1 tbsp coriander

seeds 1 tbsp cumin

seeds

½ tsp pigeon peas/thuvar

dal 1 tsp bengal

gram/chana dal 4 dried red

chillis

Method:

1. Wash, dry and top and tail the okra and cut in two.

2. Soak every one of the elements for the glue (with the exception of the coconut) in some boiling water for 15 minutes. Mix to a fine glue with the coconut and keep aside.

3. In a non-stick container, heat two tablespoons of oil over a medium fire and pan fried food the okra for 2 - 3 minutes. Sprinkle a tablespoon of water over it and cover briefly. Open top and mix again for 3 - 4 minutes until it turns somewhat fresh and dim brown. Keep aside.

4. Add this to the beaten yogurt, mixed glue asafetida powder and stew over a medium fire for 3 - 4 minutes, mixing gently.

5. Heat oil in a pot, pop the mustard seeds.

6. Wet the curry leaves and pound them in your palm. Stir

And add the other fixings rest to the sauce and combine tenderly as one. Eliminate and serve.

LENTIL EGGPLANT CURRY

kathirikai rasa vangi

Vangi is the Marathi name for brinjals or eggplants. The taste is akin to sambar with a stronger flavor of coriander seeds. And, of course, the pitlai podi does this trick.

Lentil Eggplant Curry

Ingredients:

½ cup pigeon peas/thuvar dal

2 tbsps chick peas/kabuli chana

½ kilo little eggplant

1½ tsps tamarind sauce

¼ tsp turmeric powder 1½ tbsps pitlai powder 6 curry leaves

½ tsp salt

For The Seasoning:

¼ tsp mustard

seeds 1 tsp oil

Method:

1. Soak the pigeon peas for 15 minutes in steaming hot water and cook in 2½ cups of water to a squash. Then again, pressure cook for a whistle, lower fire and cook for 7-8 minutes.

2. Soak and break up the chick peas in extremely hot water for two hours and cook over a medium fire until delicate. Keep aside.

3. Cut off the stem and hack the vegetable into 3D squares. On the off chance that not cooking promptly, drop the cleaved pieces into water.

4. Boil some water, salt and turmeric powder in a profound pan.

5. Drain water from the vegetable and add to the bubbling water. Cover and stew for 6-7 minutes or until delicate however firm. Set aside.

6. Heat oil and pop the mustard. Add the vegetable, cooked lentil, cooked chick peas, tamarind mash, *pitlai powder and salt and stew over a medium fire for three to four minutes or until the sauce thickens*. Wet the curry leaves pulverize them in your palm; mix and remove.

Tasty Tip: Sauté the eggplant in a tablespoon of oil before cooking in water.

SPECIAL SPICY SOUP

mysore rasam

A popular rasam that is generally ready by culinary experts for some a happy meal.

Mysore Rasam

Ingredients:

¼ cup pigeon peas/thuvar dal

1 tbsp tamarind purée

A touch of turmeric powder

A spot of asafetida/hing powder

¼ tsp salt

Prepare A Coarse Powder With:

1½ tsps coriander seeds

1 tsp bengal gram/chana dal

8 peppercorns

2 tsps coconut,

ground 1 tsp oil

Method:

1.Cook the lentil in 1½ cups of water until soft. On the other hand, pressure-cook for a whistle, lower fire and cook for 10 minutes.

2. When the strain diminishes totally, open and use.

3. Roast the coconut for 10 seconds or until light brilliant and set aside.

4. Heat the oil and dish the bengal gram gently, adding coriander seeds and peppercorn in a specific order. Keep aside.

5. In a profound dish, heat up the tamarind sauce, turmeric powder, asafetida powder and salt in 1½ cups of water. Stew over a medium fire for four minutes.

6. Add the mixed flavors to the rasam and cook for two or three minutes. Add the soft pigeon peas and two cups of water to the rasam and heat to the point of boiling over a low fire, or until it froths over.

7. Melt the ghee in a little dish and pop the mustard seeds. Decorate the *rasam.*

Tasty Tip: Add the shell of the wood apple for an exotic flavor. Discard it later.

GOOSEBERRY PICKLE

nellikkai urugai

This pickle is a hit with both Tamilians and Keralites. It is a somewhat unpleasant custom made pickle. The huge green gooseberry assortment is utilized for this pickle.

Gooseberry Pickle

Ingredients:

1 lb gooseberry, lemon-sized

1 tsp cayenne pepper/stew powder

½ tsp turmeric

powder 3 tsps oil

¾ tsp salt

Powder:

½ tsp fenugreek seeds

1½ tsps asafetida/hing powder

½ tsp oil

Dry meal fenugreek until browned.

Heat oil and mix the asafetida powder in it for 5 - 6 seconds.

Powder the two flavors and keep aside.

For The Seasoning:

¼ tsp mustard seeds

½ tsp oil

Method:

1. In a pan, heat two teaspoons of oil, add the gooseberry, mix and close the cover for two minutes. Open top, mix again and eliminate from flame.

2. Cool the gooseberry and de-seed tenderly, utilizing a blade. On the other hand, bubble it in water for four minutes until it is somewhat delicate. The portions self-destruct in an ideal division in your grasp, making it simple to dispose of the seeds. Keep aside.

3. Heat the oil and pop the mustard seed; add turmeric, stew powder, gooseberry and salt and mix briefly. Add the mixed flavors and mix for two minutes until well mixed.

4. Since this pickle isn't firmly seasoned with bean stew powder and oil it doesn't remain very long.

5. Refrigerate and utilize it inside two weeks.

Tasty Tip: In the South, asafetida blocks are preferred to the powder. The resin blocks emit a stronger flavor. Substitute a bead-sized piece from the block for a teaspoon of the powder. Heat half a teaspoon of oil and roast the asafetida blocks. Crush them into small pieces with a spatula so that the insides are roasted as well. Now powder and use.

SUMANGALI PRARTHANAI

Sumangali Prarthanai is an amazing and euphoric occasion summoning the favors of young ladies who died. By respecting ladies who left behind unfulfilled dreams, one feel honored and fulfilled. Ladies are officially welcomed home and the men in charge join for the lunch meeting at the end. It is performed when a girl in-regulation enters her new home and when a child or a girl is getting hitched. Sumangali prarthanai is performed on anytime besides on a Tuesday or a Saturday.

Generally, seven wedded women and two youngsters (ideally underneath the age of 10) are welcome to take part in the capacity, to share the banquet and get thamboolam, which is a pack with an entire coconut, betel leaves, betel nuts, entire turmeric pieces and an organic product (an apple or two bananas). The arrangements for this current women's capacity are critical, as it is performed with a lot of responsibility and commitment. I recall in the times of the past, the occasion started the past evening. We would go to every individual's home furnished with a little can of oil and little bundles of turmeric powder, vermilion powder, blossoms, betel leaves, nuts, and shikakai powder (shikakai is a customary Indian hair care item well known as a characteristic option in contrast to different cleansers and shampoos. The word shikakai means "organic product for hair"). These things were given over with the new garments for every last one of the invitees. The following day, they turned up new after an oil shower, dressed superbly well in a nine-yard sari. The whole function turned out to be gorgeous, filled with a lot of fun and gaiety! Even today, the tradition carries on, but minus the home visits. Not at all like the samaradhanai feast, clerics don't direct this capacity. Rather it is the senior women of the family who assume responsibility. The youthful to-be lady of the hour in whose honor the entire occasion is performed praises the welcomed women by applying turmeric and vermilion glue to the legs of the women, drawing customary examples. The unique menu arranged for the event is very like that of a samaradhanai feast. Dishes can be changed, as we can browse an enormous assortment of local vegetables and spices.

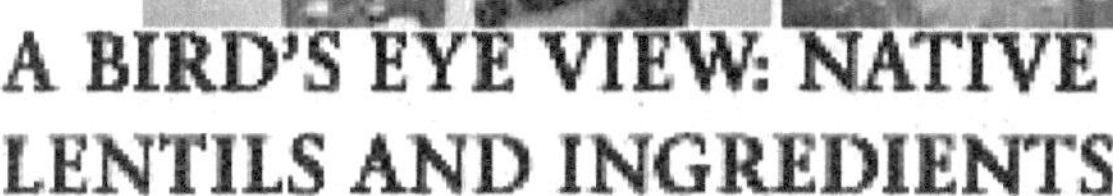

A BIRD'S EYE VIEW: NATIVE LENTILS AND INGREDIENTS

All local vegetables have been all around represented and managed in their particular sections. Go through them cautiously to acquire a reasonable comprehension of the dietary patterns and ways of life of Tamil households.

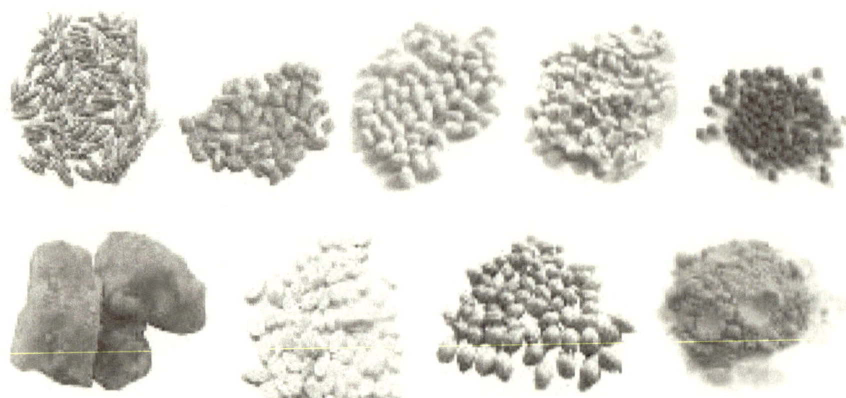

The principal picture on the top column shows CUMIN SEEDS or JEERA, a generally utilized tasty zest having a ton of therapeutic properties. It is utilized in each style of Indian cooking. Continuing, the subsequent picture is FENUGREEK SEEDS/METHI, a solid flavor that leaves an unpleasant desire for the mouth. It has high therapeutic properties and is generally utilized in Tamil cooking. BLACK GRAM/URAD DAL is known as ULUTHAM PARUPPU in Tamil. It is involved husked and entire in making hitter for pancakes/ dosas, and husked and split to be browned in gravy and sautéed dishes. MUSTARD SEEDS/RAI are utilized consistently in South Indian food for preparing. Heat a teaspoon of oil or ghee in a pan and add the mustard. Take care to close the top of the dish as the seeds will generally jump out while popping and can cause gentle consumes. Continuously add the other fixings recorded for the flavoring when the mustard starts to pop. JAGGERY/GUR, first picture on the base line, is a coarse, dark

natural sweetener produced using molasses. It comes in strong structure or in powdered structure. It is generally utilized in pastries. Sesame seeds/until (white) taste nutty. In South India they are toasted or and powdered to be added to curries/flavors and to plan confections with jaggery.
CORIANDER SEEDS/DHANIA are a fundamental fixing in sambar powder. Simmered and coarsely mixed, they are utilized as a

delightful flavor for shallow-seared vegetables and curries.
TURMERIC POWDER/HALDI is one of the most adaptable of
flavors. It is utilized as a poultice for wounds, as a moisturizer to give
skin perfection and, as a routinely involved shading and seasoning
specialist in food. It helps in battling numerous illnesses. It is an
imperative fixing in Indian Ayurvedic cooking.

RED GRAM/PIGEON PEAS/THUVAR DAL is light yellow in
shading. It is involved husked and parted in Indian cooking.
BENGAL GRAM/CHANA DAL is utilized in flavors and, or, with
jaggery to turn out delicious sweets. Bengal gram floor (besan) adds
surface and ties well. Besan goes about as a thickening specialist for
most flavors. HUSKED SPLIT GREEN GRAM OR MOONG DAL is
marginally yellow in shading. A conventional lentil in Indian food, it
is either sautéed or steam cooked in southern food and added to
sauces to give it a healthy flavor. Green gram is utilized without the
green skin in all South Indian dishes. Be that as it may, green gram
with the skin is powdered and utilized as a spice to apply on the skin
and hair. This lentil cooks quicker and has a gentle and hearty flavor.
It is a protein-filled lentil that adds to solid absorption. South Indian
rice, dissimilar to the basmati assortment, is short grain

and unmistakably appropriate for all South Indian dishes. Dark
PEPPER/KALI MIRCH is a produce of India. It has superb
Ayurvedic properties and is utilized entire or coarsely ground in
vegetables and tidbit dishes in South India. Dark pepper is more
normally utilized in Indian cooking than white pepper. INDIAN
CHILI POWDER/CAYENNE PEPPER/CRUSHED RED PEPPER is

quite
spicy. It is used as flavoring for many curried dishes and stir-fries.
DRIED RED CHILI/ SOOKHA MIRCH is a regular feature of Indian cooking.
It is more commonly used in daily South Indian fare. FRESH GRATED
COCONUT, toasted or blended with spices, is a regular in Tamil homes.
It is an indispensable part of the cuisine and the Southern culture.
Below is the green chillis dried and made into chilli flakes.

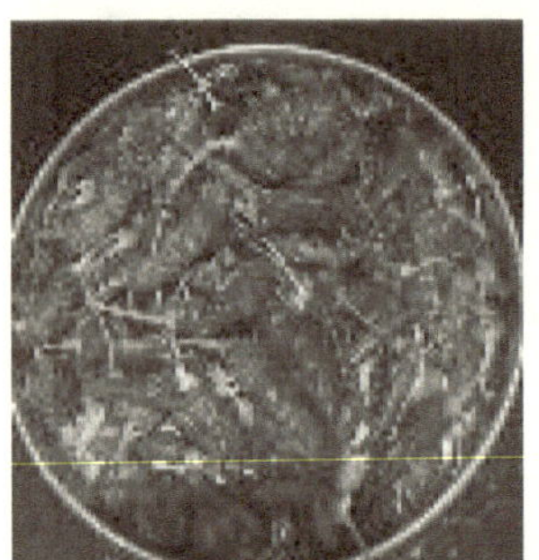 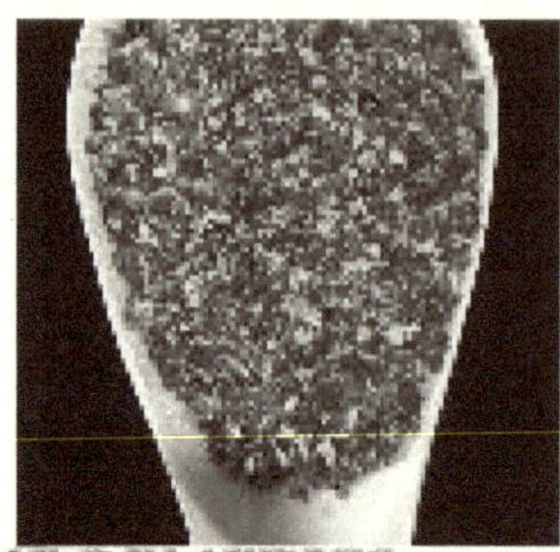

GRANDMA'S HOME REMEDIES

paati kai vaidhyam

WHEN THE DIET IS WRONG, A MEDICINE IS OF NO USE.   AT

THE POINT WHEN THE DIET IS CORRECT, THE MEDICINE IS OF

NO NEED.

--An old ayurvedic proverb

*They say, "When it comes to home remedies, grandma knows best".
Another proverb goes thus: "A life free from diseases is wealth without
limits". These are oft quoted homilies in any home or family. Even
today, home medicines prescribed by our very own physicist—a great
aunt or a grandmother—can never be ignored. Persistent and stubborn,
they give examples of the undisputed efficacy of home medicines. For a
toothache, grandmother says, "Get out the clove oil"; for a sore throat,
she recommends, "Heat some water and add pounded black pepper and
basil". Thus goes her endless menu of cures for every ailment with a
surety that proves to be her bible. She had grown up seeing her mom
and her grand- mom practice the same thing. She firmly believes that*

allopathic medicine has chemicals that cause side effects. Much of grandmother's medical truths are based on two things: her pure common sense and her ancient knowledge of herbs and their amazing cures. These remedies are inexpensive and very effective with no known adverse side effects.

My generally excellent companion Chandra Sankar brings out little books every year managing some conventional data on old Shiva sanctuaries, goddesses, legacy locales, customary haircuts and grandmother's home cures. These books were sent free to every one of her companions toward the start of the year. Chandra had brought out books 1, 11 and 111 on home cures. These are books on incredible blends called "Paati Kai Vaidyams" (grandmother's home fixes) that were composed and contributed by Mrs Leela Sekhar, Mrs Haimavathy Ammal, and Mrs Annapoorni Viswanathan. These are valid jewels without a doubt. Much obliged to you Chandra.

I quote a few cures from the primary book accumulated by Mrs Leela Sekhar,
who as of late died at the ready time of 92.

ARTHRITIS

Mix one section honey with two sections tepid water and a little teaspoon of cinnamon powder and make a glue. Gradually rub the hurting part of the body with this glue. You will see the aggravation subside in a moment or two.

Arthritis patients might take one cup of water with two tablespoons of honey and one teaspoon of cinnamon powder morning and night every day. Whenever taken consistently, this mixture can even assistance fix ongoing arthritis.

ASTHMA

To treat the side effects, add 30 - 40 tulsi (basil) passes on to four or five cups of water; strain the leaves and drink the water through the day.

BEAUTY AIDS

Mix equivalent volumes of glycerin, rose water and lemon juice. Keep in a container and apply on face, arms and legs to saturate your skin and keep it delicate and smooth. To restore dry skin, use gram flour blended in with new cream, a touch of turmeric powder and a couple of drops of lemon juice. For slick skin, use milk rather than cream.

For a compelling face pack, blend sandalwood glue with a touch of turmeric powder and a couple of drops of lemon juice. Apply on face for 15 - 20 minutes and wash with water. Shoe glue ought to be newly made at home.

Tomato juice, cucumber squeeze and dried orange strip powder can likewise be applied for a solid gleaming skin.

To carry shimmer to your eyes, add a couple of drops of lemon juice in a glass of water and sprinkle your eyes with it. It may shrewd a little yet see the result.

To reinforce the hair attaches and to dispose of dandruff, rub lemon juice on the scalp subsequent to oiling the hair. Leave in the event that for 20 minutes and, wash as usual.

Amla/gooseberry is excellent for hair. Assuming you have diminishing or falling hair, eat a couple of each day. You can bubble six gooseberries in some milk till they are delicate. Eliminate the seeds and crush into mash. Apply on the hair roots and leave for 20 minutes prior to washing. Gooseberry contains the most elevated amount

of Vitamin C and can be taken crude, in juice structure, as chutney or as a zesty or improved pickle!

BLOOD PURIFIER

Make a glue of 20 delicate neem leaves, five peppercorns, a spot of cumin seeds to be taken toward the beginning of the day at regular intervals. You might add a tablespoon of water to thin the paste.

BLOOD SUGAR

Bitter gourd adds to keeping a beware of blood sugar.

CHOLESTEROL

Make a glue of honey and cinnamon powder, apply on bread, on wheat flapjacks or on rotis; have routinely for breakfast. It positively decreases cholesterol levels.

Papaya is one more organic product with authentic characteristics: it assists with diminishing cholesterol levels and whenever taken every day, keeps the stomach in incredible working condition.

Garlic lessens cholesterol, controls circulatory strain, manages glucose and converts into a diminished danger of cardiovascular failures and heart illnesses. Garlic is extremely helpful for bringing down sharpness and furthermore goes about as a blood purifier. A characteristic anti-infection with against contagious and hostile to bacterial properties, it is said to diminish the danger of cancer.

Consuming the juice of ginger, lemon and honey can ease shortcoming because of blood pressure.

COLD/ COUGH/ SORE THROAT

Infants and youngsters (90 days to three years) experiencing extreme virus might have upset rest because of nose blocks. To work with an undisturbed rest, here is a way: take a couple of saffron strands and a piece of turmeric. Blend the expected amount of water and toil these on a shoe crushing stone into a glue and apply on the temple and around the nose of the impacted child.

For grown-ups who have extreme chest clog, here is a simple stunt to deliver the mucus. Dry dish wheat grain in a skillet and bind in a slender cloth.
Apply this poultice to the patient's chest.

Boil some basil leaves, a couple of squashed cloves, a little piece of squashed ginger and a couple of dark peppercorns in water till the blend becomes dull brown.
Add a little honey, the juice of a large portion of a lemon and taste it steaming hot. This gives speedy help from colds.

A couple of basil leaves bubbled in water for the principal cup of tea in the first part of the day, taken consistently, is great for the heart and forestalls continuous colds.

Those experiencing normal or extreme colds should accept one tablespoon of tepid honey with a quarter teaspoon of cinnamon powder every day for three days. This interaction helps fix ongoing hacks and colds and clears the sinuses.

CONSTIPATION

Turmeric bubbled in milk alongside figs helps in soothing constipation.

DIARRHEA

Two immense spoonfuls of honey given consistently can handle looseness of the bowels in youngsters (three years or more). Lemon tea likewise helps.

Take powdered dark myrobalan or Indian nerve nut (known as kadukkai in Tamil), and blend it in with some honey. A quarter teaspoon of this powder taken in three dosages is really great for the runs and diarrhea in kids over three years of age.

EYE CARE

Make a glue of nutmeg and cow's milk. Apply this glue round the eyes consistently prior to hitting the sack to capture diminishing eyesight.

For help from torment/blushing/bothering in the eyes, bubble potatoes well in adequate water. Pound this and apply round the eyes through a poultice. Do it two times per day for a compelling result.

GASTRIC COMPLAINTS

For alleviation from gas, drinking ginger pieces absorbed honey will help.

HEADACHE CURE

Mix 2 teaspoons of turmeric powder, a couple of saffron strands and a quarter teaspoon of dry ginger powder with a little water. Heat in a spoon until tepid. Apply the glue in the brow. Rehash if necessary.

Mix a large portion of a teaspoon of pepper powder and a large portion of a teaspoon of turmeric powder with 3 oz of water and drink this elixir to mitigate your headache.

INDIGESTION

For distress in the stomach, the prompt cure is to heat up some oregano/omam and beat cumin in water. Add a little stone salt, a couple of drops of lemon squeeze and drink the solution.

Heat three-fourths of some water, adding a teaspoon of beat cumin. Mix and pass on to bubble for a few minutes. Eliminate and strain cumin seeds out. Add honey. Drink this fluid rather than water. It helps.

Fry neem blossoms with explained margarine/ghee adding salt and bean stew powder to taste. Blend this in with steamed rice and eat. This helps extraordinarily for heartburn and nausea.

LOSS OF MEMORY

Boil washed bacoba/vallarai/brahmi leaves with green gram until delicate. Add salt and bean stew powder and eat it consistently basically for a month to further develop your memory power.

SKIN INFECTION/ ALLERGIES/ ITCHING

To treat tingling all around the body brought about by sensitivities, apply heavenly debris/vibhuti over the tainted piece of the body. This gives help a sluggish fix, yet a definite one.

A handy solution for rashes and bubbles is to crush neem blossoms and a teaspoon of sesame seeds, adding next to no water. Apply over the tainted parts. This will get the puss out inside three to four hours. On the off chance that the principal portion doesn't work, it ought to be repeated.

ULCERS—STOMACH AND OR MOUTH

A glue made from two almonds, two cashew nuts and a couple of poppy seeds blended in with a little milk offers extraordinary help from mouth/stomach ulcers.

The leaves of dark nightshade/macoy singed with ghee and blended in with rice ought to be eaten double seven days for a considerable length of time. This aides in restoring mouth ulcers. On the other hand, these leaves cooked with green gram and eaten with rice day by day or on substitute days assist with getting alleviation from mouth ulcers.

WATER PURIFIER

A couple of basil leaves dropped into drinking water will absolutely get the job done by decontaminating the water.

VEGETABLES A LOVELY
THOUGHT AND CONCEPT

Above you see BROAD BEANS, RADISH, TARO ROOT (COLACASSIA) and SNAKE GOURD all developed at home.

Have you at any point imagined to you concerning the wondrous sensation of seeing the veggies fill in your own home? It is simple, it is helpful and it is wonderful to be a characteristic piece of nature. Mother Earth loves us to feel the dirt with our legs and with our hands. It's a finished joy to watch it develop every day and when it is fit to be culled and cooked. It's a simply new natural life sans composts and sans pesticides. The dire need of the day - we HAVE to support the natural eco-surplus of the planet that we are living in. Our understanding and energy in developing our own vegetables products of the soil helps in going far in safeguarding our earth. We own it. Allow us to deal with it. So to the more youthful age I say 'start drawing nearer to nature!' presently. Have your own kitchen fertilizer and make great rich compost for your plants. It isn't super complicated and everything is incredibly straightforward. Do figure out how to be independent and self-autonomous. The best way to guarantee bliss, harmony and compassion to surrounding us.

www.ingramcontent.com/pod-product-compliance
Lightning Source LLC
Chambersburg PA
CBHW030308160726
47992CB00005B/1922